I've seen the results in couples Phil and Priscilla have worked with using [this] guide. You will find hope, healing, and restoration for your broken relationships. *Savage Marriage Study Guide* could be the miracle you've prayed for!

—Norm DuBois, Lead Pastor, East Coast Believers Church

Marriage doesn't have to end because of secrets and shame, but it does have to change. *Savage Marriage Study Guide* shows you how.

—Dwight Bain, Nationally Certified Counselor, Executive Coach, Author

If you and your spouse can relate to the feeling of not having it all together but posturing through life (and marriage) as though things are better than they really are, you'll be inspired by the lessons learned in Phil and Priscilla's transforming journey. *Savage Marriage Study Guide* will take you deeper into your own story.

—David Robbins, President & CEO, FamilyLife

We've seen Phil and Priscilla impact hundreds of couples in their local area and many more nationally through our ministry. In *Savage Marriage Study Guide*, you will gain wisdom and understanding of the principles and truths they went through and adopted as the foundations for their renewed relationship. You will discover true freedom, hope, and healing for your marriage.

—Paul and Niki Speed, Whatever it Takes Ministries

Savage Marriage Study Guide will help struggling marriages and also be a valuable resource for marriage counselors and pastors who want to share with troubled couples an authentic example of how God can resurrect marriages on the brink of destruction.

—Mark Merrill, President, Family First, Author of *Lists to Love By for Busy Husbands*

I'm very hopeful that *Savage Marriage Study Guide* will be used far and wide by couples who need resurrection and introduced as a significant part of authentic marriage groups in the church.

—David Loveless, Executive Director of Campuses & Leadership Development, First Baptist Church of Orlando

In the *Savage Marriage Study Guide*, Phil and Priscilla shine a light on powerful principles that can bring hope and restoration in the toughest circumstances. Their desire to help couples make their relationships right and live open, transparent lives is a model for us all.

—Jay Fechtel, President, The Fechtel Company, Director of C12 Group

SAVAGE MARRIAGE

STUDY GUIDE

SAVAGE MARRIAGE

STUDY GUIDE

OVERCOME YOUR PAST. FIGHT FOR YOUR FUTURE.

PHIL AND PRISCILLA FRETWELL

Savage Marriage Study Guide
Copyright © 2022 Phillip and Priscilla Fretwell

All rights reserved. No portion of this book may be reproduced, stored in a retrieval system, or transmitted in any form or by any means, except for brief quotations in printed reviews, without prior permission of the author.

Requests and correspondence may be submitted by email to: info@savagemarriageministries.com

Some names and details mentioned in this book have been changed to protect the privacy of the individuals involved.

The authors are not licensed marriage or mental health counselors, and this book is not intended as a substitute for advice from those professionals. The reader should consider consulting with appropriate licensed professionals in matters relating to their marriage relationship.

Scripture quotations, unless otherwise indicated, are taken from the Holy Bible, New American Standard Bible. Copyright © 1960, 1971, 1977, 1995, 2020 by the Lockman Foundation. All rights reserved.

Scripture quotations marked TPT are from The Passion Translation®. Copyright © 2017, 2018, 2020 by Passion & Fire Ministries, Inc. Used by permission. All rights reserved. ThePassionTranslation.com.

Scripture quotations marked ESV are taken from the *ESV® Bible (The Holy Bible, English Standard Version®)*, Copyright © 2001 by Crossway, a publishing ministry of Good News Publishers. Used by permission. All rights reserved.

Scripture quotations marked GNT are from Good News Translation® (Today's English Version, Second Edition). Copyright © 1992 American Bible Society. All rights reserved.

Scripture quotations marked NLT are taken from the *Holy Bible*, New Living Translation, copyright © 1996, 2004, 2015 by Tyndale House Foundation. Used by permission of Tyndale House Publishers, Inc., Carol Stream, Illinois 60188. All rights reserved.

Content Editing by Jen R. Miller at wordswithjen@writersroot.com
Cover Design by Faceout Studio, Jeff Miller
Authors' photo by Shane Valentine
Interior design and typeset by Katherine Lloyd, the DESK

ISBN: 979-8-9855402-3-9 (Print)

Printed in the United States of America

10 9 8 7 6 5 4 3 2 1

To God,
by whom everything we have learned
was made possible to experience.

CONTENTS

Acknowledgments xi
A Note from the Authors xiii
For Small Group Leaders xv

Session 1: **The Two Roads** 1
    Session 1: Homework Assignment 14

Session 2: **Wounded No More** 21
    Session 2: Homework Assignment 37

Session 3: **Overcoming the Lies of the Enemy** 41
    Session 3: Homework Assignment 52

Session 4: **The Savage Helper** 59
    Session 4: Homework Assignment 72

Session 5: **Experiencing Spiritual Intimacy** 73
    Session 5: Homework Assignment 89

Session 6: **Creating Emotional Intimacy** 91
    Session 6: Homework Assignment 101

Session 7: **Cherishing Your Spouse** 103
    Session 7: Homework Assignment 113

Session 8: **Becoming a Giver, Not a Taker** 115
    Session 8: Homework Assignment 128

Session 9: **Becoming Battle Partners** 133
    Session 9: Homework Assignment 142

Appendix A: Two-Minute Takeaways and Action Plans 147
Next Savage Steps! 151

ACKNOWLEDGMENTS

Savage Marriage Study Guide includes insights, questions, and stories contributed by many couples who attended our small groups. Their input helped our continuing refinement of this guide for others seeking God's healing for their marriages. Although space doesn't allow us to mention everyone by name, there are a few people who were particularly instrumental in helping us create this curriculum.

Paul and Jenny Speed, founders of Whatever It Takes Ministries Inc., helped us find healing and restoration in our marriage. God used their testimonies of humility, openness, and brokenness to place us on a journey of freedom and healing. It's marvelous for us to serve as volunteers at their conferences and events. Some insights in *Savage Marriage Study Guide* developed from what we learned at their weekend intensives for couples, men, and women. Jenny passed away in 2019. She lives on in eternity with our Lord Jesus, our memories, and our words in this study. We're grateful to Paul and Jenny for their leadership, mentoring, and friendship.

We thank Doug and Wendy Gohn, longtime dear friends, for leading Savage Marriage small groups at their church for many years. Their encouragement and insights into *Savage Marriage Study Guide* helped shape this book.

Thank you to our editor, Jen R. Miller, who provided countless hours of advice, encouragement, and guidance. We couldn't have done it without her.

Finally, we are so blessed by our five children and three children-in-law: Anna Hope, Becca, Tim and Johanna, Shawn and Sarah, and Michael and Chelsea. Their forgiveness for the pain we caused them was instrumental in our healing. It's wonderful to see how they've turned their pain into insight, maturity, and victory over their respective challenges. We're so appreciative of their encouragement. Our journey with them continues to be truly invaluable times of revelation for us all.

A NOTE FROM THE AUTHORS

Every marriage goes through seasons of ups and downs. If you desire to set a foundation to weather or recover from the storms of life, *Savage Marriage Study Guide* will help you and your spouse improve your spiritual, emotional, and physical intimacy. You'll experience God's healing power as you learn how to be honest, open, and transparent.

You'll gain even more from this study by participating with a small group of married couples on the Savage Marriage journey. Some couples may be dealing with past traumas, while others may be trying to develop more marital intimacy. While some of the introspection may be painful, it's important to remember that your past shaped how you think, feel, and act. Understanding how your past affected you can help you change your present circumstances.

> *You have to go backward to go forward.*

At the beginning of each printed session is an excerpt from our book *Savage Marriage: Triumph over Betrayal and Sexual Addiction* to help you visualize how God can use the principles in your marriage. If you are doing this study as part of a small group, your group leaders will be adding their stories, and we encourage you to share your stories during group time. We've found that shared stories create richer experiences essential for adding depth to what you're learning.

We realize that some parts of this study guide are very frank and may even feel offensive. Our objective isn't to shock but to help readers buried in shame who think they're the only ones with similar problems. When we share our story with groups, some listeners ask, "How are you able to be so open in sharing?" The answer is easy: God's grace took away all our shame. There's no longer reason for us to hide in the shadows.

We believe the concepts you'll learn in this study will move you toward healing, regardless of where you are in your marriage and spiritual journey. You will not only get to know your spouse better but more importantly, you'll get to know God better.

Savage Marriage Study Guide is not based on clever words, activities, or manipulation of your emotions. This study is rooted in the power of God to change your life when you come before Him humbly, acknowledge your weaknesses, and ask for His help. Anything short of these reduces *Savage Marriage Study Guide* to simply another self-help book.

> *We've found that the solution for marital conflicts isn't self-help but God-help.*

We are not pastors, theologians, or licensed marriage counselors; we're simply a couple who love and delight in the Word of God. Our experience with Christ on our savage marriage journey made us believers in marriage healing and transformation. All we have to offer is our story and our desire for God to use our testimonies through the power of the Holy Spirit as He sees fit.

If you're participating in this study, our prayer is that God will use our story to rescue, redeem, and invigorate your marriage. We've seen Him do supernatural things in our marriage, and we believe He can work the same miracles in yours. We pray you will be open to receiving His transformative grace, love, forgiveness, and counsel.

Phil and Priscilla Fretwell

Learn more about our story in our book
Savage Marriage: Triumph over Betrayal and Sexual Addiction,
available on Amazon.

FOR SMALL GROUP LEADERS

Thank you for leading a Savage Marriage small group! You're embarking on a journey to help change group members' lives while reinforcing your marriage.

Many Savage Marriage group members have said this was the most impactful group they had ever attended. Couples have found they can move forward in their marriages, spiritually and emotionally healthy, from struggles with conflicts, infidelity, addictions, sexual immorality, and wounds.

We appreciate your commitment and dedication to helping other couples overcome the trials and challenges of marriage—a journey worth taking!

ACCESS SMALL GROUP LEADER TRAINING AND OTHER RESOURCES

Leaders should access the Savage Marriage Ministries website (savagemarriageministries.com) and review the tab for small group resources. The website has materials that are updated periodically, including:

- additional activities and teaching points you can incorporate into your small group meetings;
- podcasts that complement teaching points in *Savage Marriage Study Guide*; and
- videos that you and your group members can access.

We encourage you to attend the couples', men's, and women's weekend intensives offered by Whatever It Takes Ministries (witministries.com). These power-packed weekends help solidify an understanding of the concepts presented in *Savage Marriage Study Guide* and provide the next steps for group members who want additional help in their marriages. We frequently serve as coaches at the intensives and would love to see you there!

TRANSPARENTLY TELLING YOUR STORY IS ESSENTIAL

While *Savage Marriage Study Guide* provides excellent teaching points, the real power in your small group experience will come from your testimony of what God has done in your marriage. When you openly share your marriage struggles, the transparency of your small group will increase significantly. Don't expect group members to be more vulnerable than you. For that reason, you will need to reach deep and ask God to help you share your imperfections. Being transparent about your own failures and weaknesses will enable you to recognize and know God's power at work in you like the apostle Paul experienced.

I am glad to boast about my weaknesses, so that the power of Christ can work through me. (2 Cor. 12:9, NLT)

If you're unsure how much to share about your savage marriage journey, we encourage you to read our book *Savage Marriage: Triumph over Betrayal and Sexual Addiction.* It tells our restoration story and provides an example of how to share transparently.

GROUP MEMBERS

The optimal group size is three to five couples, plus you as the leaders. We suggest you talk with each couple before the first meeting and confirm that they're a good fit for the group.

- Refer them to the Savage Marriage Ministries website (savagemarriageministries.com), and encourage them to watch the testimonials.
- Ensure they know what the study covers and how potentially transparent the group can become.
- Confirm that they're committed to attending all meetings, and inform them that each meeting is approximately two hours.
- Confirm that they're committed to completing each week's reading and homework, and inform them that the assignments will take about two hours each week.
- Each session builds on the previous, so attending every meeting is important. Please arrange a "catch-up" with participants who must skip a meeting. If they miss more than three meetings, they should restart the study with another group.
- Before each meeting, homework from the previous session should be completed and participants should read the new material and answer the questions, preferably with their spouse.
- During group time, you'll review the homework from the previous session and discuss the material for the new session. Participants will also be developing "Two Minute Takeaways" that become part of their action plan for healing and restoration.
- The homework requires participants to complete some questions individually, but the real benefits come when they transparently share their answers. Even when the homework activities generate sensitivities (that may make them want to quit), they should ask the Holy Spirit to help them work through the emotions. It's an essential part of God working in their marriage.

INTRODUCTORY AND CONCLUSION MEETINGS

Although *Savage Marriage Study Guide* includes nine sessions, you may want to schedule an introductory meeting before the first session and a conclusion meeting after Session 9.

The objectives of the introductory meeting are to

- help everyone get to know each other;
- consider an icebreaker (your own or, for example, the Savage Marriage rock, paper, scissors championship: each person plays best two out of three, and then winners advance to the next round until an overall winner is determined);
- discuss the overview of *Savage Marriage Study Guide*;
- share what God has done in your marriage; and
- discuss expectations and commitments for the group.

Your objectives for the conclusion meeting are to

- review homework from Session 9;
- ask group members to share their New Identity Statements;
- discuss their final action plans; and
- pray for one another.

If Session 9 will be your final meeting, group members should be ready to discuss their completed Session 9 homework and share their New Identity Statements at that meeting.

If you decide to hold the introductory and conclusion meetings, your small group will require eleven rather than nine total meetings. Our experience has been that holding the extra two meetings is worth the additional time investment.

SESSION 1: THE TWO ROADS

Excerpt from *Savage Marriage*

Phil

For the first twenty-eight years of our marriage, my sexual immorality was slowly numbing our relationship. We went through all the motions (working, raising kids, and going to church), but real joy and true intimacy were elusive. My sin had created a huge conflict inside me because I was a leader in our church and trying hard to achieve and manage my perfect image. I wanted to be free from the inner turmoil, but I was afraid if people knew what was going on inside me, they would no longer love or respect me. I believed that lie.

I tried men's accountability groups, apps on my computers and phone, and counseling. Nothing worked. I sank deeper into despair, but I felt God tugging at my heart, telling me He could heal my mind, help me control my behaviors, and transform my thinking and desires.

My pride problem demanded I keep everything secret. After all, no one truly knew me, and I'd already confessed my sin to God. But later, I realized that if I honestly wanted healing and freedom, I'd have to put pride down and open my secret double life to others.

So, I confessed everything to Priscilla.

Not long after, I confessed my sin to my kids and other family members. I shared all the pain of my past, wounds from long ago, and lies I had believed.

Priscilla and I prayed for God to heal my mind and us—and He did. I felt free for the first time.

Priscilla and I discovered that being honest, open, and transparent—HOT—led us to a place of humility and placed us on the road of true spiritual intimacy with God and each other.

Spiritual intimacy was the key to reviving our marriage.

Priscilla

On the outside, I looked like I had it all together. I homeschooled our five kids, attended church, and went on mission trips. But on the inside, I was a desert—empty, depressed, angry, and living with fear and bitterness.

Looking back at our marriage, I see now that it was mediocre, but I had accepted that status quo. We didn't have any real spiritual or emotional intimacy, and I thought this was what marriage was like. There wasn't enough pain to motivate me to change. I thought I could continue to live like that for the next thirty years.

When Phil came clean, I felt sucker-punched—I hadn't seen it coming. I felt betrayed, rejected, hopeless, and consumed by fear that moved into overdrive. My perfect life had shattered—all gone. Our marriage had been based entirely on lies, and I didn't have anything else to hold on to.

I cried out to God, and He showed up in an amazing way. It was the first time I heard God speak to me.

I had wanted God to fix Phil, but God said He wanted to fix *me*: my apathy, fear, anger, and bitterness. He wanted to rid me of it all. That was the beginning of change in my heart, thoughts, and life.

Like so many people, I had settled for a mediocre marriage, a mediocre life, and a mediocre relationship with God. Even though I knew I wasn't living the life God had promised me in His Word, I didn't think I was going to hell. Somehow, I was living in a third choice, on middle ground, a third option for life where I wasn't doing great, but I wasn't doing terrible. Everything was just mediocre, and there wasn't enough pain to change.

I saw how wrong I was—how wrong Phil and I were to have settled for a lukewarm, mediocre life, neither of us experiencing God's greatness or His devastating judgment. Although we had settled for the middle ground, God had so much more for us. To receive His best meant we needed to be real about who we were on the inside, strip off our pride, and walk with Him in truth and humility.

1. THERE ARE ONLY TWO ROADS

> Enter through the narrow gate; for the gate is wide and the way is broad that leads to destruction, and there are many who enter through it. For the gate is narrow and the way is constricted that leads to life, and there are few who find it. (Matt. 7:13–14)

The Bible describes many situations with only two options: heaven or hell, right or wrong, light or darkness, sons of God or sons of Satan, belief or unbelief, truths or lies. As we see in Matthew 7:13–14, there are only two roads—the wide and the narrow—and our choices and goals place us each on one or the other.

The road you choose determines what you experience.

In the above verses, the Greek word for "life" is *zoe*,[1] used in various New Testament passages to mean a current physical life or eternal spiritual life. Many people, including Christians, choose the wide road leading to the destruction of their earthly lives. Even though they may have eternal life when they die (if they have received Jesus's sacrifice for their sins), their earthly lives are less than God's best.

The two roads are evident in marriages. About half (including Christian marriages) wind up on the destructive road leading to divorce. The wide road kills marriages, demolishing lives, families, and dreams. Many people (including Christians) choose the wide road of destruction, never experiencing all the goodness and abundance God has for them.

---

[1] www.biblestudytools.com/lexicons/greek/nas/zoe.html

The alternate road for marriage is the narrow road that offers life—God's unity, peace, joy, fulfillment, and contentment—resistant to challenging circumstances and produces testimonies to family, friends, and coworkers.

"The Two Roads" diagram is an anchor chart for Savage Marriage. We'll frequently refer to the diagram throughout this study.

We may also occasionally ask: Which road are you on? This question is also good to ask yourself in the middle of marital conflicts.

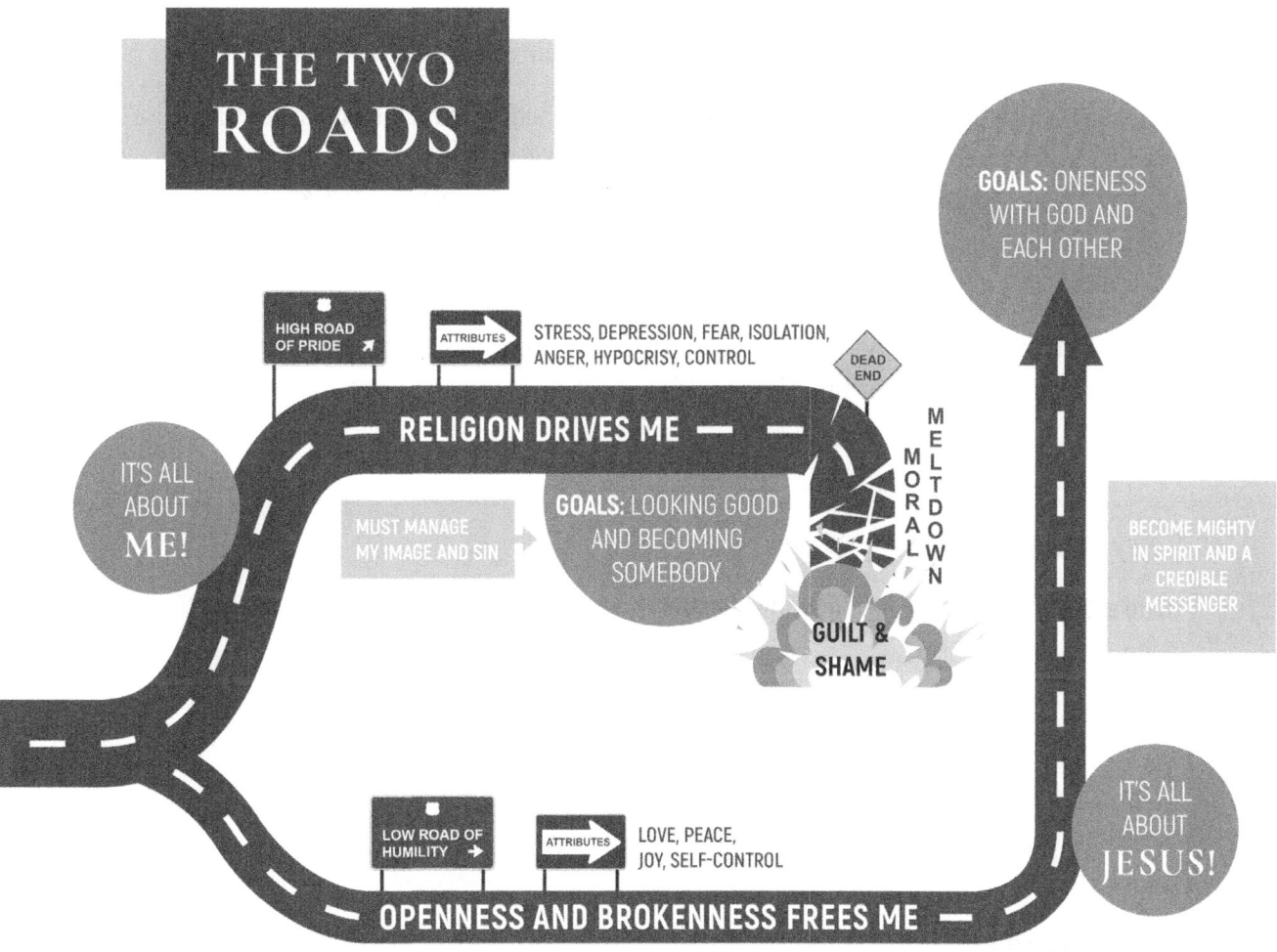

Graphic created by Krasimir Gedzhov, adapted from Whatever It Takes Ministries teaching resources

Although the diagram title is "The Two Roads," some people believe there's a middle road. They live between the two roads, going back and forth depending on their circumstances, creating an imaginary middle road. They don't believe they're proud but admit they need more humility. They typically see themselves as superior. They love the temporal pleasures of life while trying to create an appearance of godliness. They are double-minded.

There is no middle road. Everyone is *primarily* on either the wide or narrow road. The wide road is the high road of pride, and the narrow road is the low road of humility. The road you're on is based on your choices and perhaps your goals for life, and it determines how you react to relationship challenges, particularly with your spouse.

For example, you can determine which road you're primarily on based on how you *most often respond* when you have a conflict with your spouse.

The High and Wide Road	The Low and Narrow Road
You blame your spouse	You consider why you could be wrong
You defend yourself	You seek constructive criticism
You hide your weaknesses	You disclose your weaknesses
You use words of contempt to accuse and belittle your spouse	Your words bring peace and reconciliation
Your thoughts and actions promote *your* well-being and desires	Your thoughts and actions promote your spouse's well-being and desires
You point out what your spouse does wrong	You point out what your spouse does right
Your thoughts and actions reflect pride and self-righteousness	Your thoughts and actions reflect humility and openness

The key objective of this study is to move you from the high road of pride to the low road of humility and help you stay there. Living in humility enables you to persevere under marital trials and overcome victoriously.

🗝 Key Thought:

There are only two roads in life: the **wide** road that leads to **destruction** and the **narrow** road that leads to **life**.

Which road are you on, and how do you know?

2. PRIDE VERSUS HUMILITY

Do not love the world nor the things in the world. If anyone loves the world, the love of the Father is not in him. For all that is in the world, the lust of the flesh and the lust of the eyes and the boastful pride of life, is not from the Father, but is from the world. (1 John 2:15–16)

Very few people equate the boastful pride of life with the lusts of the eyes and flesh. In fact, most people acknowledge their pride, and accept it is a normal (and unchangeable) part of life. But the root of pride is the reason for most of the dysfunction, conflicts, and unforgiveness in marriage. Pride sets you on the high and wide road of destruction and keeps you there.

Pride tells you that your spouse is completely to blame for all your problems, and pride makes it difficult to see your own sin. Pride robs you and your spouse of the ability to seek mutual solutions to your marital conflicts.

"God is opposed to the proud, but gives grace to the humble." . . . Humble yourselves in the presence of the Lord, and He will exalt you. (James 4:6–10)

Renouncing roots of pride is the most important step you can take to set you on the low road of humility, toward a life of freedom, abundance, and unity with God and your spouse. To help address your marriage problems, you have to begin by looking at your pride, regardless of how much you feel your spouse is totally to blame for your relationship challenges.

ACTIVITY: PRIDE AND HUMILITY

1. Read the following verses on pride, and circle phrases that show the results of pride.

Pride:

- Prov. 6:16-17, GNT— "These six things the Lord hates . . . a proud look."
- Prov. 8:13— "The fear of the Lord is to hate evil; pride, arrogance, the evil way."
- Prov. 11:2— "When pride comes, then comes dishonor."
- Prov. 13:10— "Through overconfidence comes nothing but strife."
- Deut. 8:14— "Your heart will become proud and you will forget the Lord your God."
- Prov. 15:25— "The Lord will tear down the house of the proud."
- Prov. 16:5— "Everyone who is proud in heart is an abomination to the Lord; be assured, he will not go unpunished."
- Prov. 16:18— "Pride goes before destruction, and a haughty spirit before stumbling."
- Ps. 10:4— "The wicked, in his haughtiness, does not seek Him. There is no God in all his schemes."
- Prov. 29:23— "A person's pride will bring him low, but a humble spirit will obtain honor."
- Gal. 6:3— "For if anyone thinks he is something when he is nothing, he deceives himself."
- James 4:6— "But He gives a greater grace. Therefore it says, 'God is opposed to the proud, but gives grace to the humble.'"
- 1 Peter 5:5— "Clothe yourselves with humility toward one another, because God is opposed to the proud, but He gives grace to the humble."

2. Read the following verses on humility and circle the phrases that show the results of humility. These verses create a stark contrast between a life of pride versus humility.

Humility:

- Ps. 25:9— "He leads the humble in justice, and He teaches the humble His way."
- Ps. 147:6, ESV— "The Lord lifts up the humble; He casts the wicked to the ground."
- Ps. 149:4— "The Lord takes pleasure in His people; He will glorify the lowly with salvation."
- Prov. 11:2— "When pride comes, then comes dishonor; but with the humble there is wisdom."
- Prov. 16:19— "It is better to be humble in spirit with the needy than to divide the spoils with the proud."

- Prov. 18:12— "Humility goes before honor."
- Prov. 22:4— "The reward of humility and the fear of the Lord are riches, honor, and life."
- Prov. 29:23— "A humble spirit will obtain honor."
- Isa. 57:15— "For this is what the high and exalted One who lives forever, whose name is Holy, says: 'I dwell in a high and holy place, and also with the contrite and lowly of spirit in order to revive the spirit of the lowly and to revive the heart of the contrite.'"
- Isa. 66:2— "I will look to this one, at one who is humble and contrite in spirit, and who trembles at My word."
- Mic. 6:8— "What does the Lord require of you but to do justice, to love kindness, and to walk humbly with your God?"
- Zeph. 2:3— "Seek righteousness, seek humility. Perhaps you will remain hidden on the day of the Lord's anger."
- Matt. 18:4— "So whoever will humble himself like this child, he is the greatest in the kingdom of heaven."
- Matt. 23:12— "Whoever humbles himself shall be exalted."
- James 4:6— "Gives grace to the humble."
- 1 Pet. 5:6— "Therefore humble yourselves under the mighty hand of God, that He may exalt you at the proper time."

What did you see in this activity? Having so many verses together reinforces how important it is to understand the perils of pride and hope of humility.

Jesus was very patient with the immoral but ruthless with the proud and self-righteous. In fact, He reserved some of His harshest words for the Pharisees, the religious leaders of the day, who were self-absorbed and focused on how others saw them. (Refer to Luke 18, the Pharisee who said he was glad he wasn't like the tax-gatherer, and Matthew 23, Jesus's warning about the Pharisees.)

The Bible provides many examples of how much God abhors pride:

- Satan cast out of heaven. (Isa. 14:13–14)
- Adam and Eve cast out of the garden. (Gen. 3)
- Jesus said the Pharisees would receive "greater condemnation." (Luke 21:47)

In contrast, God recognizes, restores, and exalts the humble, such as Moses, one of the Bible's greatest leaders.

The man Moses was very humble, more than any person who was on the face of the earth. (Num. 12:3)

Moses grew up in Pharoah's palace, in a position of honor and respect. So how did he become the humblest person on earth with that aristocratic background?

The famous old-time preacher D. L. Moody said, "Moses spent forty years thinking he was somebody; forty years learning he was nobody; and forty years discovering what God can do with a nobody."[2]

Moses's forty years in the desert were the key to his humility. Desert experiences help rid us of pride and create humility so God can use us.

---

2 "Top 250 D.L. Moody Quotes (2022 Update)", Quotefancy, accessed March 17, 2022, https://quotefancy.com/d-l-moody-quotes.

In the Old Testament, God humbled people who didn't obey Him. In the New Testament, God directs us to humble ourselves. Humility is the main characteristic of life on the low road. Humility reflects Jesus' character living inside us.

Have this attitude in yourselves which was also in Christ Jesus, who, as He already existed in the form of God, did not consider equality with God something to be grasped, but emptied Himself by taking the form of a bond-servant and being born in the likeness of men. And being found in appearance as a man, He humbled Himself by becoming obedient to the point of death: death on a cross. For this reason also God highly exalted Him. (Phil. 2:5–9)

Notice in the verse that even though Jesus was God, He didn't grasp equality with God but emptied Himself, showing His humility, even to the point of death on the cross. And notice that God exalted Him!

Because of the privilege and authority God has given me, I give each of you this warning: Don't think you are better than you really are. Be honest in your evaluation of yourselves, measuring yourselves by the faith God has given us. (Rom. 12:3, NLT)

We shouldn't grasp (promote, hold on to, magnify, or rely on) anything that causes us to think more highly of ourselves than we ought. Our jobs, money, possessions, intellect, and family can all be sources of pride. Instead, we should let go of things that provide a sense of temporary importance, which pales when compared to the eternal significance God places on believers.

Then Jesus exclaimed, "Father, thank you, for you are Lord, the Supreme Ruler over heaven and earth! And you have hidden the great revelation of your authority *from those who are proud* and think they are wise and unveiled it instead to little children. ²⁶ Yes, Father, you've chosen this gracious plan to extend your kingdom. (Matt. 11:25–26, TPT, emphasis added)

Some people never receive a revelation from God's Word because they're full of pride. Humility is the key to spiritual truth being revealed in your life.

What is humility? Is it thinking that you're just a worm, good for nothing? No! Humility is seeing yourself and thinking of yourself exactly as God does—no more and no less. After all, you're an overcomer through Jesus! You stand in His righteousness at all times! That doesn't sound like a worm.

Thinking of yourself as a worm is another form of pride. Many who think less of themselves are afraid to talk in groups, fearful of using their God-given authority, and scared of being noticed. Why? Because they believe they'll be seen as a failure or ridiculed. This mindset is also pride.

Pride feeds our craving to be seen, whether as a martyr for pity or a hero for admiration.

There's a balance: seeing yourself as God sees you (no more and no less) and doing what God wants you to do—not because *you want to*, but because *God wants you to*.

Pride and humility both start in your thinking (your view of yourself), travel to your feelings (the desire to exalt yourself or God), and wind up in action (your behaviors).

Examples that describe pride:

- Thinking you're more important than others and self-sufficient
- Desiring to show your strength, possessions, accomplishments, and power for recognition and esteem
- Pursuing behaviors to mask your weaknesses and promote self-sufficiency, appearing as though you have it all together

Examples that describe humility:

- Desiring to exalt only God's power working through you so others will see His supernatural power
- Pursuing behaviors that expose your weaknesses and need for God so others will see your authenticity
- Being courageous to talk in groups from the confidence and authority that brings glory to God without regard for what people think about you

Humility is always the answer, including when times are tough and reconciliation seems impossible. You don't need clever words or better counseling; you need humility before God and then your spouse, which positions you to receive God's grace you so desperately need.

Key Thought:

God actively resists the **proud** but rescues, restores, and exalts the **humble**.

What's an area of pride your spouse thinks you need to change?

3. PRIDE LEADS TO ISOLATION

The root of all isolation is pride. Isolation allows us to hide our deepest feelings while meditating on how unjustly we were treated, frequently creating bitterness toward our spouses and others.

Many marriages on the high road move toward isolation rather than oneness during conflicts. For some couples, isolation (with no communication or sex) lasts for months while they struggle to resolve disagreements. Rather than being humble and transparent about their thoughts and feelings, they run toward isolation, hoping their spouses will sense their pain and be the first to apologize.

> "I am praying not only for these disciples but also for all who will ever believe in me through their message. I pray that they will all be one, just as you and I are one—as you are in me, Father, and I am in you. And may they be in us so that the world will believe you sent me." (John 17:20–21, NLT)

God wants us to be one with each other in the same way Jesus and the Father are one. Oneness is intimacy that's uninterrupted by isolation.

He Himself has said, "I will never desert you, nor will I ever abandon you." (Heb. 13:5)

God's character doesn't embrace isolation, and neither should we.

When couples have conflicts, they sometimes choose to separate, which creates further isolation. While there may be good reasons to separate (for example, situations involving abuse), separation makes it difficult to find time to communicate.

We encourage couples to stick together, even in the face of pain (not involving abuse). Physically seeing your spouse, and facing your emotional pain every day, creates more moments of restorative struggle that lead to contemplation and possible reconciliation. Yes, the struggle can be really hard, but you're more likely to reach a faster resolution than when you're separated.

> *There's no way to have true oneness with your spouse through isolation.*

During conflicts, you must be transparent by letting your spouse know what's going on inside you emotionally. You can't do this when you're isolated.

Intimacy can be defined as "into-me-see," the first step of humility on the low and narrow road. True intimacy will move you toward oneness with God and your spouse and away from isolation.

Key Thought:

Every marriage is moving toward either **oneness** or **isolation**.

How has isolation affected your marriage?

4. HUMILITY REQUIRES REVEALING

This is the message we have heard from Him and announce to you, that God is Light, and in Him there is no darkness at all. If we say that we have fellowship with Him and yet walk in the darkness, we lie and do not practice the truth; but if we walk in the Light as He Himself is in the Light, we have fellowship with one another, and the blood of Jesus His Son cleanses us from all sin. (1 John 1:5–7)

Enjoying true intimacy requires uncovering all secrets. Your "take it to the grave" list needs to be revealed in full to your spouse: hidden sin, past wounds, shame, and lies you've believed.

It takes humility to reveal weaknesses, and pride is the biggest obstacle to sharing who you truly are. But vulnerability has the power to create intimate fellowship, break down walls of bitterness, and heal the shame buried for years.

The life of Jesus was on full display for all to see. He had no hidden sin or shame. He had amazing fellowship with others walking in the light and no fellowship with hypocrites, such as the Pharisees. He challenged them with harsh words and later told His disciples:

"Beware of the leaven of the Pharisees, which is hypocrisy. Nothing is covered up that will not be revealed, or hidden that will not be known. Therefore whatever you have said in the dark shall be heard in the light, and what you have whispered in private rooms shall be proclaimed on the housetops." (Luke 12:1–3, ESV)

Revealing means uncovering what is hidden. You must be honest, open, and transparent (HOT) with your spouse.

> *A HOT relationship has the power to transform marriages from mediocre to marvelous!*

How do you know if you're being completely HOT?

- An honest spouse gives a factual answer; however, they may carefully parse and manipulate their words, like a lawyer, without openness and transparency. They may not technically be lying, but neither are they sharing everything you want to know. They're honest but not open or transparent.
- An open spouse, without transparency, gives you all the truthful information you want, even when you don't ask the right questions. They don't manipulate their answer or neglect something important just because you didn't ask a particular question. And instead of answering an unclear question, the open spouse may say, "I think what you want to know is . . ." However, they may only share in response to the questions rather than offering additional facts and topics. In other words, they're honest and open but not necessarily transparent.
- In addition to being honest and open, a transparent spouse wants you to know what's going on in their thoughts and emotions, even when you don't ask questions. A transparent spouse desires *into-me-see* that doesn't require you to be a good interviewer.

If you want to have a truly intimate marriage relationship, you always need to be HOT, showing (and allowing) honesty, openness, and transparency.

Many of us wear masks because we're afraid we won't be loved when people see who we truly are. We hide our authenticity, pretending we have perfect lives. Masking was first evident in the Garden of Eden after Adam and Eve sinned. They hid from God and used fig leaves to cover themselves. But God didn't want *them* to cover their sin—*He* wanted to cover them to show His unconditional love.

He called out to them, "Where are you?" because He wanted them found. No hiding. He then killed animals (a sign of Jesus's death to come for the covering of sin) and gave them the skins to cover themselves. But to wear God's provision for their sin, they first had to remove their man-made provision for sin—the fig leaves. In other words, they had to uncover, reveal, and show who they authentically were underneath. They had to become HOT with God and each other.

To experience God's healing, we must do the same—uncover our secrets, shame, and guilt. We must remove our human efforts (fig leaves) to manage and cover up our sin and shame by coming clean with our spouses about everything we've been too proud or afraid to share. You may feel like what you've done (or what's happened to you) makes you weird or perverted, but all temptation is "common to mankind".

(1 Cor. 10:13) To get rid of your shame and find real intimacy with your spouse, you will have to share your story. In Savage Marriage, groups members have shared many secrets with their spouses, including infidelity, porn, rape, molestation, incest, bestiality, abuse, fantasies, and flirting. All of these things are common.

You might be surprised to find fantasies and flirting on this list, but all infidelity starts with flirting, and the precursor to flirting is always fantasizing. To get these things out of our minds, we have to come clean with them.

You may wonder how your spouse will react to knowing everything you've done, everything that's happened to you, and everything you've been thinking about. You may even be fearful of sharing your past. Here's hope: we have not seen anyone walk away from a spouse who was truly HOT, humble, and broken. Humility has amazing power to restore relationships, form powerful bonds, and take you to an entirely new level of transparency. That's what we're praying for you.

> **Key Thought:**
>
> You must be HOT **(honest, open, and transparent)** to have **intimate fellowship**.
>
> What do you need to share with your spouse to be fully HOT?

5. HUMILITY IS REQUIRED FOR BROKENNESS

The sacrifice you desire is a broken spirit. You will not reject a broken and repentant heart, O God. (Ps. 51:17, NLT)

Psalm 51 was written by King David after he repented from his sin with Bathsheba, wife of Uriah the Hittite. As described in 2 Samuel 11–12, King David had sex with Bathsheba, and she conceived a child. To cover up his sin, King David had Uriah killed on the front lines of battle.

When confronted by the prophet Nathan, King David admitted his sin and later chronicled his repentance in Psalm 51. In that poignant psalm, his humility and brokenness drove him to cry out to God for cleansing and restored joy—a picture of how God wants us to respond when confronted by our sin.

Being broken means your soul is crushed and torn over your sin, almost to despair. Sometimes when people sin, they're sorry about the circumstances they've found themselves in but not necessarily broken before God. Brokenness is a deep sorrow caused by seeing the significance of your sin before a holy God rather than sorrow caused by the pain you felt or caused.

For example, the children of Israel were in bondage in Egypt for four hundred years, but it wasn't until the end that they cried out to God.

The sons of Israel groaned because of the bondage, and they cried out; and their cry for help because of their bondage ascended to God. (Ex. 2:23)

Even though the children of Israel had been slaves for four hundred years, it took that long for them to become truly broken. Groaning under their oppression, they cried out to God.

God had waited for their bondage cry even though He knew they were suffering. Then, immediately, the scene shifted—God spoke to Moses and put His plan for deliverance in motion:

"The cry of the sons of Israel has come to Me; furthermore, I have seen the oppression with which the Egyptians are oppressing them. And now come, and I will send you to Pharaoh, so that you may bring My people, the sons of Israel, out of Egypt." (Ex. 3:9–10)

God may be waiting on your brokenness and humility in marriage. He sees your pain, suffering, and abuse, but He's waiting for your bondage cry.

> *You can be HOT without being broken,*
> *but you can't be broken without being HOT.*

 Key Thought:

Brokenness is evident in a **bondage cry** for God's supernatural grace and healing.

Have you ever cried out to God in brokenness? Describe what happened.

6. HUMBLE CONFESSION LEADS TO HEALING

Confess your sins to one another, and pray for one another so that you may be healed. (James 5:16)

Many people believe we must confess our sins to be forgiven by God. But that isn't what the Bible teaches. When we're humble and broken before God and accept His gift of salvation, we're born again in Christ and forgiven for *all* sin—past, present, and future.

While confession is a crucial part of repentance (a complete turning away from sin), confession is not God's requirement for *forgiveness*. He forgave us our sins when Jesus took *all* our sins upon Him on the cross (Heb. 10:14). If confession is required for forgiveness, people would be frantically trying to confess all their sins on their deathbeds and habitually through life. Consider how many times you sin each day, each hour, remembering that sin begins in your heart, with your thoughts. Praise the Lord Jesus Christ that we do not have to live in that bondage but are *free* from sin by *faith* in Him! When we're "born again" (salvation, 1 Peter 1:3) in Christ, we are made new (2 Cor. 5:17), are clothed, and can stand in His righteousness (Isa. 61:10; Eph. 4:24), fully forgiven for our sinful nature and all sin (Heb. 2:10).

So why confess our sins?

James 5:16 instructs us to confess our sins to be healed—not forgiven. When we sin, we damage our souls (mind, will, and emotions) and our relationships with God and need healing. Our souls need healing as much as our bodies! However, instead of confessing sins, we sometimes wear masks and hope that somehow, with enough time, our pain and trauma will just go away without anyone knowing what we've done. The damage doesn't simply go away with time. Thereby, many people are living unhealed, though forgiven.

But shouldn't we confess our sins to God?

Yes! When we talk to God about our sins, the Holy Spirit moves us toward healing and confession of our sins to others. Many Christians repeatedly confess their sins privately to God but don't receive healing until, in humility, they confess their sins to others as well.

Some confess their sins to others like reading the newspaper or repeating a religious statement—an unemotional, unbroken description of their sins. Confession should always come from a broken and contrite heart. After confessing to their spouses, they may ask, "Do you forgive me?" They may even tell their spouses, "You have to forgive me because that's what Jesus commands us to do." This type of confession and "forgiveness" rarely produces the real fruit of healing or the times of refreshing referred to in Acts 3:19:

> You must repent and turn back to God so that your sins will be removed, and so that times of refreshing will stream from the Lord's presence. (TPT)

"Times of refreshing" represent the emotional healing of your soul that comes from confessing your sins in broken repentance. A confession may at first create pain in you and your spouse, but broken repentance will ensure that times of refreshing will eventually come.

Pride will lead to the briefest confessions with the fewest details and least discomfort. Pride refuses to revisit previous confessions and demands that spouses "forgive and forget."

Humility will exude a broken spirit and contrite heart eager to confess all relevant details. A spirit of true humility is willing to revisit all previous confessions and answer as many questions—honestly, openly, and transparently—as the spouse may have. Humility gives up all demands for forgiveness and takes complete responsibility for all actions. Humility can unlock the power of brokenness and vulnerability that can create a brand-new marriage relationship on the low, narrow road to healing and abundant life.

Key Thought:

You must be **HOT** (honest, open, and transparent) to be **healed**.

Have you ever experienced a moment when confession led to the healing of emotions or a damaged relationship? Describe what happened.

After the group session, turn to Appendix A and complete your Two-Minute Takeaway.

Session 1: Homework Assignment

1. In the *unshaded* boxes, mark any statement that describes how you generally think, feel, or act. The statements represent the true you, so you'll be marking according to how you authentically think about yourself and see yourself and how you believe others may honestly see you—*not* how you *want* people to see you.

   Don't mark a box if you think a statement doesn't describe you honestly. Usually, your first impression will be correct, so don't overthink the statements. Try to complete this exercise in three to five minutes.

No.	Description	A	B
1	When confessing sin, I confess specific details.		
2	When I confess sin, I speak in generalities.		
3	I accept personal responsibility and see where I'm wrong.		
4	I'm compassionate toward others.		
5	I'm concerned only with how God sees me.		
6	I'm concerned with appearing respectable and defending my reputation.		
7	I'm concerned with how my material possessions compare to others'.		
8	I'm concerned with what others think.		
9	I'm content to live within my God-given limitations.		
10	I'm defensive when corrected.		
11	I'm eager to make others a success.		
12	I am easily offended, hold grudges, and have emotional temper tantrums.		
13	I'm elated when praised and deflated when criticized.		
14	I'm motivated to serve others.		
15	I'm not concerned with who gets the credit.		
16	I'm not preoccupied with what others think of me.		
17	I'm open and transparent with others.		
18	I'm overwhelmed with my spiritual need.		
19	I'm quick to admit failures and seek forgiveness.		
20	I'm quick to criticize or blame others in positions of authority.		
21	I'm remorseful over sin only when I'm caught.		
22	I'm repentant over sin, and I take steps to forsake sin.		
23	Others see me as pretentious or unapproachable.		
24	I'm self-denying.		
25	I'm self-protective of my time, rights, and reputation.		

No.	Description	A	B
26	I'm willing to be open and transparent.	■	
27	I'm willing to yield the right to be right.	■	
28	I have a lot to learn from God and others.	■	
29	I claim and demand my rights.		■
30	I compare myself to the holiness of God and feel the need for mercy.	■	
31	I compare myself to others and feel deserving of honor.		■
32	I'm concerned with people seeing the consequences of my sin.		■
33	I continually sense my need for a fresh encounter with God.	■	
34	I desire to be a success.		■
35	I desire to be recognized and appreciated.		■
36	I desire to be seen as perfect.		■
37	I desire to be served.		■
38	I easily forgive others.	■	
39	I easily receive correction with an open and humble spirit.	■	
40	I encourage and lift up people who are in positions of authority.	■	
41	I esteem others as better than myself.	■	
42	I feel confident in how much I know.		■
43	I feel that others need revival more than me.		■
44	I find it difficult to share my spiritual needs with others.		■
45	I focus on the failures and faults of others and can point them out.		■
46	I give thanks in all things, and I'm not quick to become bitter.	■	
47	I have a demanding spirit.		■
48	I have a sense of unworthiness, and I'm thrilled that God uses me at all.	■	
49	I have a very hard time saying, "I was wrong. Will you forgive me?"		■
50	I have an independent and self-sufficient spirit.		■
51	I have not, or very few times, confessed my sins to others.		■
52	I hurt when others are promoted and I'm overlooked.		■
53	I initiate reconciliation even when the other person is wrong.	■	
54	I keep people at arm's length.		■
55	I know I have nothing in me to offer to God.	■	
56	I look down on others and think highly of myself.		■
57	I maintain control and demand that things be done my way.		■
58	I immediately attribute to God any praise I receive.	■	
59	I must prove that I'm right.		■
60	I receive criticism with an open and humble heart.	■	

No.	Description	A	B
61	I recognize my need for others.		
62	I rest and wait on God to act on my behalf.		
63	I risk getting close to others and knowing them intimately.		
64	I think of what I can do for God.		
65	I think the best of others.		
66	I try to control and manipulate others and the circumstances around me.		
67	I wait for others to ask forgiveness when there's a relationship problem.		
68	I want others to see the real me, as God sees me.		
69	I yield my rights and control.		
70	I'm self-conscious.		
71	I have a generous, giving spirit.		
72	My instinct is to cover up sin so no one finds out.		
	TOTAL (add the number of checks in columns A and B)		

2. What do you believe column A represents? _____

3. What do you believe column B represents? _____

4. What three items do you most want to change from the table, and why? (Review with your spouse and consider their point of view.)

    a. _____

    Why? _____

    b. _____

    Why? _____

    c. _____

    Why? _____

5. Given that we've all done things that showed our pride and arrogance, read to yourself the following humble confessions, and circle any you believe are true of you in your marriage relationship. Then describe in the right-hand column how this made your spouse feel. *This is very important!* While your spouse may say they forgive you, they won't feel the forgiveness unless they are convinced you understand and apologize for how what you did made them feel. The offense they took doesn't reside in your actions, but their feelings. Push into this—it's the key to making this activity meaningful!

Circle statements that apply to you:

I'm sorry because...	How did this likely make your spouse feel?
I've constantly been looking for problems in your life, and I've ignored the problems in my own life.	
I've focused on you as the cause of our problems, and I now see myself as the cause.	
I've seen our problems as caused by you more than me.	
I've not taken 100 percent responsibility for my part in the problems in our marriage.	
I've told other people that you are the problem in our marriage.	
I've thought my answers were always correct.	
I've demanded my way.	
I've not listened to you.	
I've asked you to serve me rather than me serving you.	
I've called you names, cursed, and used words to hurt you.	
I've disrespected you in front of others.	
My actions toward you have demeaned and humiliated you.	
I've put you down in front of others.	
I've wanted to show you that I'm stronger than you.	
I've made you feel spiritually inferior to me.	

I'm sorry because . . .	How did this likely make your spouse feel?
I've been selfish in bed—it's all been about me.	
I've neglected you emotionally.	
I've chosen isolation to hurt you when we argue.	
I've left you alone when you needed help.	
I've not protected you when you were in danger.	
I've let anger control me when I didn't get my way.	
I've expressed anger and contempt to hurt you.	
I've allowed my addictions to hurt our relationship.	
I've placed greater priority on my work than on our relationship.	
I've placed greater priority on other relationships than you and our family.	
I've been a hypocrite and always focused on looking good in public while never being transparent about how things truly are at home.	
I've made you keep secrets to cover up my sin.	
I've not shared my (or our) struggles and sin with you or anybody else because I was prideful and arrogant and wanted to look good and be somebody.	
I've asked God to work in your life, realizing now that He needs to first work in my life.	

6. Read your circled, humble confessions aloud to your spouse.

   For your statements to be effective:
   a. share with your spouse in more detail than you described above, and
   b. apologize for the way you made your spouse feel (you need to describe their feelings, not just say you were sorry you made them feel bad).
   c. Ask your spouse if you understood and described their feelings accurately.
   d. Be open to input from your spouse.
   e. Apologize for any feelings of theirs you missed.
   Example: "I'm sorry I haven't listened to you. I was more focused on myself than listening to what you had to say. I realize this probably made you feel unimportant and that I didn't respect your point of view. Is this the way I made you feel? I'm so sorry. Please forgive me."

Some of your confessions can bring out real pain and emotions. Ask God to help you embrace humility in your confessions and grace in your forgiveness.

7. It's understandable if you may not feel like forgiving your spouse, but you can certainly ask God to help you forgive them. Let your spouse know:
   a. you forgive them by faith, and
   b. you're asking God for feelings of forgiveness.

8. Identify areas of your life that you've kept secret from your spouse. These may be wounds from your past, shame, and hidden sin—typically the first aspects to come to mind. Embrace this opportunity to practice being HOT with your spouse.
   a. First, *pray together*. Ask God to give you each the grace and humility to share and to hear secrets. Ask Him to give you a transparent and broken spirit. To better prepare your hearts, you may decide to pray over a couple of days (depending on what you're planning to share).
   b. Then share your secrets, how they have affected your life, and how they have made you feel. Share why you've kept the secrets. Share with sensitivity, not like you're reading the newspaper.
   c. Ask your spouse how knowing your secrets makes them feel. Offer to answer any questions your spouse may have, provide any details they need, and answer all their questions, no matter how many. Answer with humility, not minimizing the impact of anything you've done, and without debating how your confessions made your spouse feel.
   d. If you share a secret that offends your spouse, humbly apologize, and ask them to forgive you for what you did and how your actions made them feel.

9. No matter what your spouse shares, tell them "Thank you for sharing," and resist the urge to criticize. If you have the same (or similar) secrets, be HOT in telling the secrets. You may have pain from what your spouse shared, but it's better to know now than two decades later. You must be HOT to be healed. This step is one of the most significant steps of freedom, healing, and restoration you can take as a couple. Don't treat this step lightly.

10. Together, review your Two-Minute Takeaway in Appendix A (that you completed during the group session), and record your spouse's observations. Write down the action steps you and your spouse agree are appropriate for the relationship.

Notes

SESSION 2: WOUNDED NO MORE

Excerpt from *Savage Marriage*

Phil

I rose early one morning, anxious about sharing wounds I had kept hidden for so many years.

Priscilla joined me shortly, sitting at the kitchen table and gesturing toward my open journal. "Looks like you've been writing a lot this morning. What's going on?"

I glanced up briefly, putting my pen to the side. "I've been thinking about our conversation about how you felt in the doctor's office during your STD test—you know, the part about how shameful you felt."

She nodded. "Tell me about it."

"I've had the same feelings of shame about wounds that go back many years, to when I was a kid, growing up with just my mom and sister. There are some things in my life I'm very ashamed of. Things I've always said I would take to my grave.

"Out of fear, I've never shared them with anyone, and I've been afraid to share them with you, fearing you wouldn't love or respect me. I know I was just a kid when the stuff happened, and I didn't even know you then, but they've demanded secrecy in my life. I shook hands with them, agreeing I'd keep them buried. But every time someone gets close to these areas, like in a discussion or triggered by something I see in a movie, I shudder and want to run and hide.

"I don't want to fear shame anymore, but I feel like the devil has told me that what I've done is uncommon, weird, perverted, and very sinful. So I've kept them hidden from everyone, including you. Now, I want to be free from the past and the power of shame more than I want to hide. I feel God wants me to start by sharing what happened to me."

Priscilla

When I caught Phil using porn ten years into our marriage, I tried to forgive and forget, believing the lie that time heals all wounds. Eighteen years later, Phil confessed his secret life. A week later, at 4 Days 2 Hope, God showed me that my earlier wounds had scabbed over, and underneath was a dangerous infection that had been continually eating at my soul, fueling my feverish anger. God began removing my scabs, and I could see the pus of unforgiveness that had been hidden and poisoning me for so long. I was awakened to realize I hadn't forgiven Phil or forgotten how his betrayal made me feel. The memory of that day was still breeding anger, resentment, and bitterness. "Time heals all wounds" was truly another lie. The truth was closer to: time causes wounds to fester.

Wounds are very sensitive parts of our lives that we tend to bury because they're painful. Every time our wounds come to mind, we cringe. We may avoid doing, seeing, hearing, or even smelling anything that could cause us to remember and feel the pain.

Being healed from wounds doesn't mean we'll no longer remember them. Healing means we can now look at our wounds, acknowledge the scars and pain, and understand how they impacted our lives.

Some impacts of unhealed wounds:

- Unforgiveness toward our abusers
- Anger and a desire for revenge or repayment
- Being overly sensitive when someone or a circumstance gets close to your wounds
- Embracing addictions that help numb the pain
- Shutting down emotionally because it's too painful to feel

Your healing process begins by identifying your wounds and pain, feeling your pain, confessing your wounds to others, forgiving your abusers, and allowing the Holy Spirit to open your emotions. Healing can allow you to be free from the wounds of your past.

1. DON'T IGNORE YOUR WOUNDS

"Come to Me, all who are weary and burdened, and I will give you rest." (Matt. 11:28)

Jesus knows wounding and pain, and He feels our pain just as He felt the pain of His wounds. He knew our lives would be full of burdens, heavy loads, and things that would weigh us down and that our traumatic experiences would produce painful wounds. Therefore, he made provision for our pain and healing. What are the results of unhealed wounds?

- A wound may cause you to continually feel the pain of the offense you suffered, even when many years have passed.
- A wound may tell you not to forgive your abusers but to punish them or hope for other revenge.
- A wound may tell you to bury the memory and numb the pain, but still, you may cringe when someone comes close to seeing it.
- A wound can still make you cry, even after decades. We've seen a woman in her late eighties crying when she talked about her ex-husband and the abuse she suffered by him over fifty years earlier because *her wound had not healed.*
- Wounds can also cause you not to see yourself as God sees you because wounds are directly related to the lies the devil wants you to believe about yourself. Lies are always contrary to what the Word of God says about you. Examples:

    - You may be fearful because of something that happened to you. But the Bible says, "Do not be afraid, Zion; Do not let your hands fall limp. The Lord your God is in your midst, a victorious warrior" (Zeph. 3:16–17).
    - You may lack confidence because someone told you that you were a failure. But the Bible says you "can do all things through Him who strengthens me" (Phil. 4:13).

- You may feel dirty because you suffered sexual abuse, but the Bible says you are the "righteousness of God in him," Christ Jesus (2 Cor. 5:21).
- Wounds can also cause you to be overly sensitive to certain topics and situations, quickly bringing out impatience and anger that may cause you to retreat into isolation. These sensitivities impact your marriage, especially when they're not disclosed fully to your spouse.
- Carrying wounds can make something relatively minor become a meltdown. Some couples handle wound-related meltdowns by sweeping everything under the rug. They think that ignoring the situation will eventually lead to healing, believing the lie that "time heals all wounds." In that mindset, people can become stuck in a pit of emotional wounds for the rest of their lives.

When your spouse is triggered into an emotional meltdown, you may not see their wound or pain because they keep them deeply buried. Instead of asking, "Why are you acting that way?" ask with gentleness, "What's happening inside you?"

Proverbs 20:5 says, "A person's thoughts are like water in a deep well, but someone with insight can draw them out" (GNT). You may be the person of insight God wants to use to help your spouse pull out deep thoughts and wounds hidden for most of their life.

It's essential to look at the emotional meltdowns in your marriage and consider whether they resulted from hidden wounds.

The good news is that Jesus offers healing for *all* wounds—yours and your spouse's. But to receive healing, you each need to go through the difficult process of identifying and exposing the wounds.

a. Ask the Holy Spirit to help you see each wound.
b. Be bold to share your wounds with your spouse and perhaps others.
c. Believe that Jesus was wounded for you and already took your wounds and weaknesses to the cross. Believing that Jesus made provision for your healing means you only need to *receive His healing*, by faith, with humility, transparency, and brokenness.

♀ Key Thought:

When you ignore the wounds of your **past**, they eventually show up in your **marriage**.

How have the wounds from your past affected you and your spouse?

2. REVEAL YOUR WOUNDS

There must be revealing for healing to occur, which means you must show someone else what's going on inside you.

In Luke 6, Jesus entered the temple on the Sabbath and saw a man with a withered right hand. In those days, people with such infirmities often became beggars, increasing their shame and despair. The right hand was typically the main working hand, so this man was probably destitute and may have tried to hide his infirmity. But Jesus wanted to heal him.

He said to him, "Stretch out your hand!" And he did *so*; and his hand was restored. (Luke 6:10)

Before the man could receive healing, he had to expose his infirmity, the root of his pain, the biggest disappointment of his life.

You may say, "I just can't expose my wounds—I'm too ashamed!"

Some people believe the man's withered hand was paralyzed, in which case he may have thought he was *unable* to stretch out his hand. So how would he have done so? Only by the power Jesus gave him was he able to thrust his hand forward into the light where the group saw his infirmity. That's the power Jesus has given you for your healing. When you feel afraid or ashamed to expose your wounds for healing, ask the Holy Spirit for boldness to step into the light. He wants you to reveal your wounds in faith and receive His healing.

> *Wounds never revealed are never healed.*

In our discussions with couples from Savage Marriage, we've seen that wounds are most often identified by what people fear, since emotional pain is associated with wounds.

Fear is quick to rise in those who believe they may encounter a circumstance that will touch or reopen their wounds, causing pain to resurface. The fear is feeling wounded again. As a result, they compensate, sometimes irrationally, by limiting their encounters. In doing so, they also limit positive experiences.

Quite a lot has been written about wounds and their impact. During our Savage Marriage small groups, the following list of emotional wounds are those most often identified. Consider whether any of the following circumstances created your wounds.

1) Fear of abandonment

About 50 percent of parents are divorced, so the fear of abandonment is common. But even in situations where parents aren't divorced, children can feel abandoned by emotionally absent parents and carry that feeling through the rest of their lives. An adult's childhood experiences can cause the individual to feel that their parents or caregivers disregarded their well-being, education, or accomplishments. The person feels they weren't valued or cared about. For example, we've heard many adults comment on how their parents never attended their sporting events or band concerts.

The wounded may attribute the emotional and physical absences to their parents' or caregivers' jobs or other commitments and may carry a sad countenance and a desire not to do that to their kids. Likewise, children who were adopted or raised in foster care often carry a sense or fear of abandonment.

People compensate for their fear of abandonment by not connecting easily to others, reasoning if they never get close to anyone, they'll never feel abandoned again. They may limit relationships to a surface level. Though many will marry, their spouses and children may wonder why the relationship can't seem to grow emotionally close and feel or see evidence of the barrier but not know the cause.

2) Fear of rejection

All of us have a deep need to feel accepted, especially by those closest to us—family, friends, social and work groups. People who carry a fear of rejection tend to avoid situations they believe could result in them feeling left out or ostracized. Even the slightest remark or look from someone can be interpreted as a rejection. Thereby, they may withhold their thoughts and be reluctant to make decisions, fearing disapproval. The likelihood of hypocrisy is high in those who fear rejection because any sense of personal defect can feel like grounds for rejection.

People compensate for their fear of rejection by taking on jobs, roles, and responsibilities that maximize their chance of success and acceptance while staying hidden in the background. They also tend to be perfectionists to minimize the risk of rejection and placate their spouses when voices raise, fearing their spouse's rejection. They're excellent followers because they'd rather not be seen or heard, and they wait on others to suggest new ideas and lead. They may also be quick to manage their image in the hope of being admired.

3) Humiliation

Humiliation is very close to the word *humility*. In Savage Marriage, we urge humility as God's desire for us. So what's the difference between humility and humiliation?

- *Humility* is voluntarily letting go of your need to be seen, admired, or exalted. It's all about your choice to place yourself at a lower level than you possibly deserve.
- *Humiliation* is when you are forced to be seen by others in *ways that feel painful* to you—incompetent, inept, inferior, unwanted. Humiliation occurs when others demean you, withhold basic respect from you, insult your dignity, or disclose things about you without your permission; when you make mistakes; and when others discover your secrets. One tragedy of humiliation is that it takes away the ability of the person to voluntarily humble themselves. For example, rather than waiting for a husband to confess his infidelity to the family, the wife lets everyone know without discussing it with the husband and giving him a chance to confess his own sin first.

4) Betrayal or fear of trusting others

Although betrayal is commonly thought of as marital infidelity, it includes any situation where someone breaks their bond of trust. For example, a betrayal of trust can occur when prior to marriage a spouse says they want children, and after marriage they change their mind. This type of betrayal can be just as poignant as infidelity. Feelings of betrayal can surface from even the seemingly small things, such as opting out of a date night in favor of spending time with a friend, a hobby, or working late. Anytime someone you trust fails to come through, feelings of betrayal can arise.

People compensate for a fear of betrayal by having an inordinate need to control others, situations, decisions, and outcomes. The rationale is that if they can control everything, they can't then be betrayed. They may check and cross-check relationships, hire private detectives, want constant reinforcement of their spouses' and children's whereabouts, and be insistent that others follow their direction. The number of questions they ask, and other demands, may be irrational, and their victims may be clueless that the root is the demander's fear of betrayal.

5) Injustice

Injustice is an undeserved action against you in any form, or the feeling of something undeserved. It could have been a terrible childhood of parental absence or of abuse or trauma by anyone or any circumstance. Injustice as absence or trauma can be felt by those who lost a parent, sibling, or other close relationship. Adults who describe their injustices tend to believe that life has dealt them an unfair hand, and they carry anger, resentment, and bitterness indicative of a desire for revenge.

People compensate for this wound by emotionally flatlining—feeling neutral or numbed in a wide variety of circumstances or as a lifestyle, tending to not show much emotion.

Jesus experienced all five wounds.

1. He was abandoned by His disciples.
2. He was rejected by the Jews and people in His hometown.
3. He was humiliated on the cross as He hung there naked.
4. He was betrayed by Judas and denied by Peter.
5. He was unjustly convicted and killed on the cross after living a sinless life.

Even though He was wounded, His victory over the wounds provides the healing for our wounds.

He was pierced for our offenses, He was crushed for our wrongdoings; The punishment for our well-being was laid upon Him, and by His wounds we are healed. (Isa. 53:5)

Jesus demonstrated on the cross what was necessary for healing His wounds and our wounds:

- He was in complete submission to the Father, humbly giving up His life in exchange for what God's will was for Him. In the same way, we need to be willing to do whatever it takes to receive healing for our wounds.
- He was completely exposed as He hung naked, which examples our need to reveal our wounds, at least to our spouses.
- The Jews wanted to humiliate Jesus on the cross by taking His life by force. But Jesus converted the humiliation to humility when He said, "Father, into your hands I commit my spirit" (Luke 23:46, ESV), clearly showing His voluntary rather than forced death. In the same way, we destroy the humiliation and shame of our wounds when we voluntarily reveal them to others and pray for God's healing to manifest in our souls.

Unhealed wounds place limitations on our lives by creating anger, fear, shame, and unforgiveness. They can also make us feel disconnected from others. Examples:

- People who experience marital infidelity may have difficulty forming another intimate relationship.

- People abused physically or sexually may have difficulty with marital intimacy.
- People subjected to verbal abuse may shut down in the face of arguments.
- People who were humiliated may have anger that causes them to abuse others.

Turning toward our wounds feels counterintuitive because they hurt. But unrevealed wounds cannot be cared for—they become infected. The first step toward healing is to bring your wounds into the light and turn toward the pain.

Key Thought:

Wounds that are never **revealed** are never **healed**.

What wounds have you experienced that still need to be healed?

---

3. DON'T BE A WOUND COLLECTOR

The following explanations (adapted) and quotes are from "On Wound Collectors" by Joe Navarro, MA, *Psychology Today,* September 6, 2015.

Wound collectors "are individuals who go out of their way to collect social slights, historical grievances, injustices, unfair or disparate treatment, or wrongs—whether real or imagined."

Wound collectors are hypersensitive to words, situations, and experiences that remind them of a previous wound. They not only are sensitive to the wounds but ignore logic by grabbing on to everything remotely close to a prior wound to reinforce the validity and pain of what they felt.

Wound collectors habitually collect more wounds by selectively looking for people and circumstances that will support their entrenched beliefs. Wound collectors

- don't forgive or forget;
- don't move on;
- wallow in the actual and often perceived transgressions by others; and
- "allow sentiments of animosity and vengeance to percolate and froth at the surface by constantly nurturing their wounds."
- "Through flawed observations, logic, or reasoning, the wound collector is hobbled by a 'confirmation bias' that systematically reinforces a pre-existing belief or position";
- is convinced of their beliefs, even in the face of contrary evidence; and
- becomes saturated and stumbled by their toxic brew of self-created irrational biases that breed hate and contempt for others—two key features abundantly present in wound collectors.

"As you can imagine, in an imperfect world where there are real injustices where people make mistakes, and stupid things are said and done, the wound collector never has to go far to feel victimized." Interestingly, even secular psychologists have concluded that collecting wounds leads to emotional breakdown and destruction.

Psychological wounding is nothing new—many people have such wounds, but most don't seek to indulge them. Though people are naturally traumatized by the cause of their wounds, most people try to put their hurts behind them. And, unlike the wound collector, most people don't seek to nourish psychological wounds.

People around a wound collector sometimes wonder why the individual gets so upset over things that seem so minor. Eventually, the wound collector's distress turns into bitterness, and someone brushing up against their wounds can produce volcanic emotional eruptions.

> See to it that no one comes short of the grace of God; that no root of bitterness springing up causes trouble, and by it many become defiled. (Heb. 12:15)

People who collect wounds gather current grievances that

- reinforce their conviction of how badly they were hurt;
- affirm (in them) that injustices did occur against them; and
- qualify (in them) their right to feel bitter.

The broader problem is that the wound collector's bitterness affects not only them but the people around them.

If you're a wound collector, it's time to get rid of your warehouse of grievances and refuse to collect more. Wound collecting is harmful to your soul and those around you. You need healing.

Key Thought:

Wound collecting can lead to **bitterness** that affects others around you.

How have you seen the impact of wound collecting in your relationship with your spouse and family? What wounds are you collecting?

---

4. EMBRACE YOUR PAIN

> And when they came to a place called Golgotha, which means Place of a Skull, they gave Him wine mixed with bile to drink; and after tasting it, He was unwilling to drink it. (Matt. 27:33–34)

After Jesus was given over to the Romans to crucify Him, they scourged Him with a whip that ripped His flesh from His body, creating terrible wounds. They gave Him wine mingled with gall (or bile) to deaden the pain, which most people would have eagerly accepted, but Jesus refused the drink. Why? He wanted to know the painful cost of forgiving and healing the world's sins. He refused anything that would numb His pain.

Jesus's refusal of the pain reliever is an important truth to remember. Our guilt and shame create pain that can push us toward unhealthy and damaging behaviors that numb our feelings (such as addictions) to cope with our pain.

Numbing builds walls in our efforts to protect ourselves from getting hurt again. But because we can't selectively turn off our emotions or a particular area of pain, numbing by any means may also shut down *all* our feelings, and consequently, we don't experience the joys of life. We may seldom cry but also seldom have a good belly laugh. It's less painful (and less fearful) to stay unemotional.

Many people have remained emotionally numb for so long that they've accepted the lie that they're not capable of emotion. Among the many people we've walked alongside, we've found that anyone who desires to change their mindset and behaviors—and allows themselves to feel pain and express the sources of their grief—can gain healing and regain their ability to feel and express emotions.

Here are examples of how people numb themselves from the emotional pain of wounds, guilt, and shame. Any of these can become addictions.

- Binging TV, computer, video gaming, phone, earbuds
- Burying in books, hobbies, or social media
- Gambling
- Overeating
- Overworking
- Overparenting
- Overspending
- Abusing alcohol and prescription medication
- Using illegal drugs
- Using porn
- Masturbating
- Isolating (from spouses and others)

Even though numbing our emotional pain is bad for us, we do it anyway. Why?

a. Numbing triggers dopamine, a brain chemical that causes us to feel better and modulates pain temporarily. While dopamine is one of God's provisions, naturally activated in times of trauma, we're not to unnaturally force it, which is abuse and overuse like anything else against our bodies (abusing food, drugs, sex, etc.). But 1 Cor. 6:19 says "your body is a temple of the Holy Spirit within you," created by our Maker and entrusted to us for safekeeping with honor and reverence.

b. We gravitate to people with similar wounds and join in their escapes, temporarily making us feel better. But 1 Cor. 15:33 says, "Do not be deceived: 'Bad company corrupts good morals.'"

c. We convince ourselves that we deserve our "guilty pleasures" because our spouses aren't treating us well. The poor conditions of our marriages is not an excuse for out-of-bounds sexual behavior and other guilty pleasures but a call of action to seek God. 1 Cor. 10:13 says, "No temptation has overtaken you except something common to mankind; and God is faithful, so He will not allow you to be tempted beyond what you are able, but with the temptation will provide the way of escape also, so that you will be able to endure it. "

d. We convince ourselves that our guilty pleasures are the "only things I have to look forward to" or "the only things that fulfill me." Whatever overly consumes our time leaves little remaining time in a day to develop relationships with our spouses. But Psalm 103:5 says that our heavenly Father "satisfies your years with good things, *so that* your youth is renewed like the eagle."

e. We escape through things that numb us because we don't want to hear from God, so we avoid facing Him. But like Psalm 103:5, the Bible is filled with passages that speak of God's abundance of good things He has for those who put their faith in Him.

🔑 Key Thought:

Choosing to **numb** emotional pain shuts down your emotions and can lead to **addiction**.

How have you chosen to numb your emotional pain?

---

5. FORGIVENESS BEGINS HEALING IN YOU

Be kind to one another, compassionate, forgiving each other, just as God in Christ also has forgiven you. (Eph. 4:32)

God's forgiveness in Christ should be reflected in you for others. You can forgive because He first forgave you. His forgiveness is a clear demonstration of His supernatural power, and that's why the world struggles with unforgiveness.

> *Healing of your wounds will always be accompanied by forgiving your offender.*

Because your wounds are attached to people who have abused you, your healing comes only after you've forgiven them for what they did and how they made you feel.

You must openly confront the source of your pain by:

1. Speaking Words of Forgiveness for Healing

Forgiveness is a spiritual act that starts with words of faith, believing that the feelings of forgiveness will manifest over time in your soul (mind, will, and emotions). Forgiveness and healing are not results of your emotions but your intentional act of will to

   a. voluntarily open your heart to God by faith to let Him heal your wounds;
   b. ask Him to help you stop making life choices based on your fear of being wounded again; and
   c. speak your pain and forgiveness to your offender.

> *Outward words in faith are always needed to begin inward healing.*

You must choose to release your emotional pain by *speaking your pain and forgiveness* to your offenders, even when you don't feel like taking this step. If you wait until you feel like it, you may wait an entire lifetime for healing. This step takes humility, which is why pride is the biggest obstacle to forgiveness and healing.

Declaring that you have forgiven your offender activates your emotional healing. In healing, you will experience freedom in your soul that you never dreamed possible. This freedom journey begins with faith.

They overcame him because of the blood of the Lamb and because of the word of their testimony. (Rev. 12:11)

Some people believe this verse means we should testify *after* overcoming our sins and wounds, but the verse says our testimonies *precede* our overcoming. God wants us to speak in faith that we *are* overcomers *before* overcoming. Therein is the act of *faith*.

To forgive an abuser (which could be your spouse), begin by declaring in faith that God *is* healing you and enabling you to release your abuser by forgiving them. Then follow up by testifying to someone else about the abuse and that you are forgiving your abuser.

2. Releasing Repayment and Revenge

We tend to believe that withholding forgiveness hurts the other person. In truth, unforgiveness hurts only us. Unforgiveness is so destructive to our lives that it can feel like torture.

Forgiving your abusers means you choose to stop demanding repayment for their wrongful deeds. In other words, you are releasing your need for revenge, an act of humility.

> *Pride demands repayment, but humility demands nothing.*

Peter came up and said to Him, "Lord, how many times shall my brother sin against me and I still forgive him? Up to seven times?" Jesus said to him, "I do not say to you, up to seven times, but up to seventy-seven times." (Matt. 18:21–22)

Jesus then told the disciples a parable illustrating that forgiveness no longer demands repayment. (Read Matthew 18:23–35.)

Forgiveness essentially means *trusting God* to deal with your abuser, and not adding your actions of revenge to hurt your offender. Even though you may not ever outwardly act on revenge, forgiveness releases the feelings of revenge that can otherwise hold you in captivity for the rest of your life. Forgiveness is about your inner freedom through faith in God's promise to make all things right in His way and time.

When you offer forgiveness, you've taken a step of humility and faith by releasing your desire for repayment and revenge in exchange for God's best for you.

Another step of humility, beyond forgiveness, is to offer your abuser a blessing. Your blessing testifies to your offender that you want God's healing in their life. Getting to that place in your heart and mind, where God enables you to bless your abuser, is a significant step in healing you and your abuser.

3. Evaluating Evidence of Forgiveness

You may struggle with knowing whether you've really forgiven someone. How do you know? Here are five identifiers that show your forgiveness is complete:

a. You no longer feel bitterness or other negative emotion when you think of your offender.
b. You no longer feel superior to your offender.
c. You no longer feel that your offender owes you something.
d. You no longer desire revenge.
e. You have moved from behaving like a victim to making the daily choice to walk in victory.
f. You no longer feel painful emotions when talking to others about your experience.

🔑 Key Thought:

You must **forgive** your past offenders to receive **healing** and **change** your present circumstances.

Who do you need to forgive, and why haven't you done it?

---

6. WHAT FORGIVENESS DOES *NOT* MEAN

a. You'll forget the offense.

"I will forgive their wrongdoing, and their sin I will no longer remember." (Jer. 31:34)

People frequently say, "God forgets our sins, so we should forget the sins against us." But in Jeremiah 31:34, God doesn't say He "forgets sin"; He says He *forgives* sin and "will no longer remember" (a choice), which is different than forgetting. We never actually forget our wounds and trauma, but healing can allow us to remember them through the lens of forgiveness and healing.

When you've offered complete forgiveness and then memories pop into your mind, you can choose to remember God's grace that allowed healing from your pain. You're no longer focusing on the pain and insufficiency of your life; you remember God's grace healing you inside. In this way, you can "remember no more" what happened to you in the past. You're not forgetting the trauma or abuse but choosing to remember it in a context of forgiveness and healing.

Even though your wounds have healed, naturally, scars remain—as did the scars in Jesus's hands, feet, and side. Like Jesus, you now see your scars as reminders of God's grace over you and in you, and the wounds are no longer painful.

b. There are no consequences for wrongdoing.

There will always be consequences for sin, even with forgiveness. For example, you can be forgiven for gambling, but you may have already lost your house. If you abused your spouse, you might have to abide by a restraining order even if your spouse forgave you.

Although wounds may be healed, there are scars of consequences that can serve as a reminder of God's grace and healing.

c. You can trust that person.

You may be reluctant to forgive your spouse because you don't think you can ever trust them again. But the fact is your trust was misplaced before their offense.

Your trust should have been only in God, who is sinless, because *trust* implies instinctive, unquestioning belief, and God is the only One who is completely trustworthy. Even the best people are human and fallible and thereby will at times let you down.

Your confidence in people will build over time based on how they show their reliability, but your *trust* should be only in God.

d. You should pretend the offense never happened.

Pretending the offense never happened, or burying it under the rug, is not a healing, restorative strategy. You may feel the need to talk numerous times about your wounds, forgiveness, and healing. But if you've genuinely forgiven your offenders, your sharing will be from a perspective of thankfulness while remembering forgiveness, victory, deliverance, and God's grace.

True forgiveness means you can talk freely about your wounds without hiding and shame. Forgiveness is experienced in your soul, and talking about your experiences through the lens of forgiveness and God's grace will help you process your emotions.

e. You're instantly healed of all emotional pain.

While forgiveness first happens in your spirit, it can take time to manifest in your soul (mind, will, and emotions). If your spouse forgives you of an offense, you have to be patient while their pain and emotions process through their soul. For example, a spouse will continually bring up their hurt, and the other spouse responds with impatience and anger, saying, "I thought you forgave me for that!"

Remember that forgiveness is different from healing. Forgiveness can happen in a moment, but healing can take time. A key part of forgiveness is showing patience and compassion when returning to the source of pain, and allowing God to heal your spouse over time.

f. There will be reconciliation.

Forgiveness isn't a magic pill that means the relationship is healed, reconciled, and back to the way it was before.

- Forgiveness occurs in *one person's* heart when they release their offender from revenge and repayment.
- Reconciliation occurs *when two people* forgive each other and then work toward restoring their relationship.

Whether or not reconciliation seems possible, you should still forgive because forgiving frees *you* from bitterness, fear, and anger. Also, your forgiveness might be a catalyst in the offender's heart toward reconciliation if they do the work needed for healing and restoration.

🔑 Key Thought:

Understanding the truths of forgiveness includes knowing what forgiveness is **not**.

What have you mistakenly believed about forgiveness?

---

7. OFFENDERS SHOULD ASK FOR FORGIVENESS

We've been talking about the wounded forgiving their offenders, but there's another side of the wounded we must look at: the wounded being a "wounder." We each have wounds, but we each have also wounded others.

> "If you are presenting your offering at the altar, and there you remember that your brother has something against you, leave your offering there before the altar and go; first be reconciled to your brother, and then come and present your offering." (Matt. 5:23–24)

When you think of your past, you may remember situations where you were the perpetrator. As the verse above says, "your brother has something against you" in situations where you were the abuser, adulterer, or otherwise the betrayer.

Being the perpetrator of a wound feels very shameful, so some people keep their sins on their take-it-to-the-grave lists. They're fearful of the reactions of others if their sin was to become known. They feel unable to confess to anyone because they're afraid of being abandoned, unloved, and disrespected. Consequently, they live in bondage to their secrets and hide to avoid others knowing. Inside, they agree with the devil that they're wicked and perverted, and they feel there's no way out.

If you were the perpetrator and still living in shame and fear, you can become free by offering a broken and humble apology to the person you've offended. An apology from true humility and brokenness has the power to help the wounded person forgive you, and for you to heal.

An apology is more than saying, "Will you forgive me?" or saying, "I'm sorry I hurt you." As an example, a powerful apology to your spouse should include the following points:

- Express your deep regret and sorrow for how your behavior affected your spouse. They should hear your regret and sorrow in your words and also see these in your countenance and body posture. In other words, your deep inward contrition and brokenness should be visible outwardly.
- Acknowledge that what you said or did (or allowed to happen) was wrong. Take complete responsibility for the offense without deflecting, rationalizing, blaming someone else, or trying to describe how hard it would have been for you to take another path.
- Show you understand how you made your spouse feel by describing their emotional and physical pain.
- Commit to not let the sin happen again, and describe the action steps you will take to control your offensive behavior.
- Request (not demand) forgiveness while acknowledging how difficult it must be to forgive (especially in situations of a repeated offense). If your spouse doesn't readily offer forgiveness, don't place them on any timetable or make them feel guilty for not forgiving you. It's your fault they're in this situation, and you have to own how you've made them feel.
- Ask your wounded spouse if there's anything you can do to provide restitution, make it right, or repair the offense. Making restitution is an important part of your apology and can convince your spouse that you're willing to do whatever it takes to heal the offense. Your commitment to follow through can lead to possible reconciliation, but your reluctance to do what they ask puts your reconciliation at risk.

When a wounded person is in fear of more emotional or physical pain, it's impossible to establish an intimate relationship. So, if you're still in regular contact with your spouse, ask what you can do to help them feel safe. The following examples of boundaries may be useful:

- Let them know at all times where you are by using a location tracking app on your phone and agreeing to never turn it off.
- Agree to always take their call or quickly return their call.
- Text them whenever you feel tempted to act on your addiction or other offensive behaviors.
- Allow access to your phone and computer history, providing all passwords and agreeing not to erase anything they want you to keep.
- Agree to always be home by a certain time.
- Agree to sleep in a separate room or otherwise maintain your distance until your spouse rebuilds confidence in you.
- Attend joint or individual counseling or small group study.
- Agree not to have lunches, dinners, or travel solely with someone of the opposite sex.
- Agree to eliminate other behaviors that make your spouse feel unsafe, like driving too fast, yelling, cursing, being physically aggressive, threatening to withhold money for needs, spending money foolishly, or using contact with your children as a bargaining chip to obtain what you want or other such emotional manipulation.

Again, for the possibility of reconciliation, you must be willing to do whatever your spouse asks to help them feel safe to reestablish their confidence.

Although the example apology and boundaries above are focused on your wounded spouse, the principles apply equally to others you've hurt.

Pride is your biggest obstacle to apologizing. The power in an apology to begin healing isn't in the information you confess but in the state of your heart from which you confess. Asking God to help you express your apology in authentic brokenness and contrition over your sin can place you on the path to healing and possible reconciliation. Even if you don't believe the person who you wounded will forgive you, humbling yourself in apology and asking for forgiveness is the right thing to do and will bring healing to your soul.

🔑 Key Thought:

A humble and contrite **apology** can move an offended person to **forgive** and possibly **reconcile** with you.

Who do you need to apologize to? What did you do to hurt them? Are you willing to apologize?

After the group session, turn to Appendix A and complete your Two-Minute Takeaway.

Session 2: Homework Assignment

1. Individually, revisit the five common sources of wounds (abandonment, rejection, humiliation, betrayal, and injustice). Describe the nature and source of your wounds. Reach deep, and ask the Holy Spirit to reveal them to you. Don't let the shame of your past keep your wounds covered and unhealed.

Source	Emotional	Physical	Sexual	Spiritual
Dad				
Mom				
Siblings				
Church				
Friends				
Others				

2. Write a symbolic letter to your most significant abusers, which could include your spouse. Use your discernment, and ask God which people you need to write to.

    Use the following suggestions to help you write the letters. Ask God to help you feel the pain of your wounds as you write to each individual.

    a. Name your abuser.
    b. Describe what they did to you.
    c. Describe how you felt when they wounded you and the impact of the wound on your life.
    d. Describe any choices you made to numb your pain.

 e. By faith, write words of forgiveness, and release your abuser to God, letting go of any need for revenge or repayment.

 f. In some cases, you may be aware of reasons in your abusers' lives that caused them to abuse you, and it would be good to acknowledge those reasons. Though you didn't cause their wounds that led them to abuse you, extend compassion by telling them you're sorry for what happened in their lives as a victim that led them to abuse you. Then write a prayer to God for them.

3. For every victim of a wound suffered, there has been a perpetrator. Ask God to reveal to you the times you have been the perpetrator. Write a symbolic letter to your victim. Use your discernment, and ask God which people you need to write to. Use the following suggestions to help you write the letters. Ask God to help you feel the pain you caused as you write to each individual.

 a. Name your victims.

 b. Describe what you did to them.

 c. Describe how they probably felt when you wounded them and the impacts the wounds may have had on their lives.

 d. Describe any choices you made to numb the pain from your guilt.

 e. Express apologies, ask God to release the victims from the consequences of their wounds, and ask the victims to forgive you.

 f. In some cases, you may be aware of the reasons that caused you to abuse others, and it would be good to explain the reasons. Write a prayer to God for each victim.

Note: When you've been the perpetrator, God may prompt you to go to the person(s) you offended or abused and express a sincerely humble apology in person. An apology offered in humility with brokenness has the power to heal and restore relationships. Ask God to lead and empower you to apologize.

4. Read your letters *aloud* to your spouse. This action is very important and a step some people omit because it can be emotionally draining. *Please press into this! Sharing aloud will provide healing for your souls!*

5. While listening to your spouse's letters, ask the Holy Spirit to help you feel their pain. Assure them that there is no longer shame or open wounds—only scars representing grace, forgiveness, and healing. For wounds created in you by your spouse, express honest words of assurance and faith that you've forgiven them.

6. Pray together, and ask God to enable you each to experience the refreshment of forgiveness and healing in your souls (mind, will, and emotions).

7. Review with your spouse your Two-Minute Takeaway from Session 2, and record their reaction and your action steps in Appendix A.

Note: If you have more than one forgiveness and apology letter to write, make copies of the templates on the following pages before writing.

Letter of Forgiveness for Hurting Me

Dear _____,

Letter of Apology for Hurting You

Dear _____,

SESSION 3:
OVERCOMING THE LIES OF THE ENEMY

Excerpt from *Savage Marriage*

Phil

The example of my dad's adultery—and, I believe, his attempted suicide—kept one fear ever before me: *You will be just like your father, destined to suffer the same fate.* With every failure through the years, that was the message the enemy whispered in my ear.

Priscilla and I had made a vow at the beginning of our marriage to never use the D-word. Yet here we were, dealing with something that had the potential to take us there.

Becoming divorced, like my father, was one thing I desperately wanted to avoid. But on the day of my confession to Priscilla, the enemy of my soul, the devil, resurrected in me his familiar refrain: "See, you're just like your father!" In my desperation to prove him wrong, I took steps toward truth, humility, and freedom.

Coming clean to Priscilla about my sin, past, and what was happening inside me (something my father had never done with my mother) gave me hope.

As memories pulsated in my head, I gained new insight, the final puzzle piece that formed the complete picture of my addiction. I clearly saw the lies I had believed:

- A little porn use is acceptable.
- Every man needs to learn how to accommodate this "normal" level of lust because it's uncontrollable.
- How can we be responsible for sin that's uncontrollable? We can't.

In truth, porn is the destroyer of spiritual, emotional, and physical intimacy—not only of the marriage but of the whole family. Allowing porn into my mind was not a victimless crime. Believing the lies had led me further into darkness, despair, and lustful desires than I had ever imagined I would go.

We're going to unpack the lies we've believed about ourselves. We label our thoughts as a lie when the way we think about ourselves conflicts with the Word of God.

ACTIVITY 1:

Watch the video "Overcoming the Lies of the Enemy" by Whatever It Takes Ministries at www.witministries.com/overcoming-the-lies-of-the-enemy. You can do this together or individually, and it's okay for your children to watch. It contains good examples of how lies come into our lives. The video is about fifty minutes.

ACTIVITY 2:

1. Read through the following list of common lies, and circle the lies you've believed about yourself.

2. For each lie, find a corresponding promise from God's Word that shows you the truth God says about you. Search the internet for Bible verses by inputting the opposite phrases into your search field. For example, if you think God doesn't care about you, search "verses that show God cares about me."

3. Note the Scripture reference(s) in each box you circled, and think about how God's truth counteracts the lies you've believed.

I'm a burden.	I'm a loser.	I'll never measure up.
God doesn't care about me.	I'm not gifted.	I'm a burden to my parents.
Everyone hates me.	God doesn't love me.	I'm not special.
I'm a failure.	I'm all alone.	I'm not worthy of love.
Everything I do turns out bad.	My opinions never matter.	I cannot keep from failing.
No one understands me.	I'm forgotten.	I'm on my own.
Nobody loves me.	I'm hopeless.	I'm stupid.
I must protect myself (or be hurt).	I'm insignificant.	No one appreciates what I do.
No one thinks I do anything right.	I'm never going to get anywhere in life.	I can't speak in public.
God never does anything for me.	Everyone is against me.	I'm ugly.
I always mess things up.	I'm not accepted.	I'm weird and different.
Nothing I have to say is important.	I'm not good enough.	I'm worthless.
I'm just a passive person.	God cannot use me.	I can never overcome _____.
I will never accomplish anything.	I can't say anything right.	I can't hear from God.
I'll never be man enough. I'll never be woman enough.	I'm not important.	No one cares how I feel.
I don't deserve anything.	I can never change.	I cannot be forgiven.
I don't have any real friends.	I'm always left out.	I can't tell anyone what I've done.
I have nothing to offer someone.	I'm an idiot.	I'm always wrong.
I can't speak well.	If I'm not perfect, I won't be loved.	I will turn out like my _____.
I'm boring.	It's always my fault.	I need to take care of myself.

I was a mistake.	I'm not qualified.	I need to be admired to be significant.
I'll never be as good as _____.	Everyone will be better off without me.	If people admire me, I'm doing the right thing.
God has no purpose for my life.	I can't please God.	I can't be successful in my career.
I'll never be free.	I don't fit or belong.	I may be homosexual.
I'm not adequate.	My past will always define me.	Nothing I do is ever good enough.
I'm not needed.	I'm not likable.	I can't be free from lust.
I'm going to turn out like my _____.	Other: _____	Other: _____

1. BE CAREFUL WHO YOU LISTEN TO

"You are of your father the devil, and you want to do the desires of your father. He was a murderer from the beginning, and does not stand in the truth because there is no truth in him. Whenever he tells a lie, he speaks from his own nature, because he is a liar and the father of lies." (John 8:44)

The devil's only real weapon is deception. He wants you to believe lies about yourself, your spouse, and others and wants you to believe that God's Word is not true and that God doesn't care. Lies keep you bound to your current circumstances and hinder you from moving forward with God.

Now the serpent was more cunning than any animal of the field which the Lord God had made. And he said to the woman, "Has God really said, 'You shall not eat from any tree of the garden'?" The woman said to the serpent, "From the fruit of the trees of the garden we may eat; but from the fruit of the tree which is in the middle of the garden, God has said, 'You shall not eat from it or touch it, or you will die.'" The serpent said to the woman, "You certainly will not die! For God knows that on the day you eat from it your eyes will be opened, and you will [a]become like God, knowing good and evil." When the woman saw that the tree was good for food, and that it was a delight to the eyes, and that the tree was desirable to make one wise, she took some of its fruit and ate; and she also gave some to her husband with her, and he ate. . . . Then the Lord God said to the woman, "What is this that you have done?" And the woman said, "The serpent deceived me, and I ate." (Gen. 3:1–6, 13)

How did the serpent deceive Eve? First, he influenced her by questioning God's words, asking if God had really said she was not to eat from any tree. Then he directly contradicted what God had said, stating that Eve would not die if she ate the fruit. He even suggested that God didn't want them to become like Him, essentially telling Eve to doubt God's motives. The serpent's words made Eve doubt whether God truly cared about her.

The serpent influenced Eve to believe lies, which led to her eating the forbidden fruit.

Believing a lie of the enemy requires three things:

1. The enemy communicates a lie.
2. We contemplate the lie.
3. We agree to believe the lie.

In other words, we collaborate with the enemy by listening to him and believing what he says. Notice when Eve reoriented her listening to God's voice, she concluded the serpent had deceived her.

> Be careful who you listen to and what you decide to believe.

In the middle of a conflict, good questions are "Who am I listening to?" and "What am I hearing?" These questions will lead you to consider whether your thoughts could be lies. If lies, you can reject them in Jesus's name and ask the Holy Spirit to lead you into all truth.

Is there anything you're deceived about right now?

There's only one correct answer: "I don't know!" Why? When deceived, you don't realize you're deceived! Our inability to recognize our state of mind when deceived is why we need to always be in a state of mind to ask the Holy Spirit to lead us "into all the truth."

"When He, the Spirit of truth, comes, He will guide you into all the truth; for He will not speak on His own, but whatever He hears, He will speak; and He will disclose to you what is to come." (John 16:13)

🔑 Key Thought:

Agreeing with the **lies** of the devil keeps you in **bondage**. Believing God's **truth** sets you **free**.

Describe a lie you've believed and how it's affected you.

2. There's a Conception to Every Lie

You weren't born with lies. Every lie begins at a definite time, either when you have an intruding thought or see, hear, or experience something contrary to God's Word and character.

We know from Acts 5:3 that the devil can interject thoughts into our minds. This concept may be hard to understand, but when Ananias sold some land, it was Satan who told him to lie about the offering.

Peter said, "Ananias, why has Satan filled your heart to lie to the Holy Spirit and to keep back some of the proceeds of the land?" (Acts 5:3)

Although it's difficult to articulate how Satan influenced Ananias to lie, we see that Satan told Ananias he could keep some of the proceeds from the land sale for himself. Ananias agreed with the lie and then acted on it.

Lies we believe may be planted through intruding thoughts or based on what we perceive as truth. For example, we live in a marketing-oriented society that influences us to believe lies about who we are, who we can be, and what we need. The central message of much advertising is lies, contrary to the Word of God, and strongly suggests that the key to a better life is acquiring their products and services. In truth, abundant *life* is found only in God's presence, when our hearts are grafted into Jesus Christ.

The one who has the Son has the life; the one who does not have the Son of God does not have the life. (1 John 5:12)

Jesus said:

"Remain in Me, and I in you. Just as the branch cannot bear fruit of itself but must remain in the vine, so neither *can* you unless you remain in Me. I am the vine, you are the branches; the one who remains in Me, and I in him bears much fruit, for apart from Me you can do nothing. (John 15:4–5)

You have to be careful what enters your eyes and ears because you can mistake Satan's schemes as things that bring fulfillment and contentment when, in truth, he offers darkness, bondage, and unrest.

Freedom from a lie requires you to identify the source (Satan) and see his distortion in what you saw, heard, or experienced.

🔑 Key Thought:

The devil lies to you through **intruding thoughts** and by distorting what you **see**, **hear**, and **experience**.

Have you ever experienced intruding thoughts? What happened?

3. Wrong Thinking Leads to Wrong Behaviors

Believing lies affects more than your thinking and feeling. Lies also affect your actions.

> *You do what you do because you feel what you feel because you think what you think.*

When your thinking is wrong, your feelings will be wrong, and your behaviors will follow accordingly. You never do anything ungodly that you haven't felt like doing, and you never feel like doing something you haven't thought about. Thereby, your thinking is linked inseparably to your actions.

You want to make your marriage better, and by this point in Savage Marriage, you may have a list of things that you or your spouse need to change. But to experience behavior change, you first need to change the way you think, which includes overcoming the enemy's lies.

> Do not be conformed to this world, but be transformed by the renewing of your mind, so that you may prove what the will of God is, that which is good and acceptable and perfect. (Rom. 12:2)

This verse focuses on changing your thinking, not your actions. Self-help books and conferences typically provide tips and techniques for changing your behaviors and encourage a renewed commitment to work harder. But eventually, you become tired of the to-do list.

To change your behaviors, you must start with changing your thinking—allowing the Holy Spirit to transform your mind through the Word of God.

> The word of God is living and active, and sharper than any two-edged sword, even penetrating as far as the division of soul and spirit, of both joints and marrow, and able to judge the thoughts and intentions of the heart. (Heb. 4:12)

The Holy Spirit uses the Word of God to judge the thoughts and intentions of our hearts, which produces conviction to change the way we think and act.

In addition to changing our thinking, we must engage our emotions to create sustainable change in our behaviors.

Most Bible studies focus on two actions: learning what the Bible says and doing what it says. When we don't do what the Bible says, the logical conclusion is that we don't know the Bible well enough. So, we may then look at the Greek and Hebrew roots and add some commentaries to help us better understand. When our thoughts and behaviors remain unchanged, we're told to memorize more Scripture or have more faith. However, the missing ingredient is that many of us know the Word intellectually and desire to change, but we haven't received the Word as a personal, direct revelation from God. Viewing God's Word as His direct communication of revelation to you personally affects your thinking *and* emotions. And the emotional impact of God's Word more significantly affects your behaviors than intellect alone.

The apostle Paul said in Ephesians 1:17 that God wants us to have "a spirit of wisdom and of revelation in the knowledge of Him."

> *When we receive God's wisdom and revelation, the Word of God engages us emotionally, which moves us toward behavior change.*

Do you remember what happened to the apostle Paul when the light blinded him? Was he affected only intellectually or also emotionally? (Read Acts 9.) Blinded, he was undoubtedly affected emotionally. He refused to eat anything until he could see again.

Pursuing God solely on an intellectual basis does not have the power to sustain continued behavior change. Only by receiving God's Word as His revelation to you directly can you see real and lasting behavioral changes in your mind *and* emotions.

> ### 🔑 Key Thought:
> Overcoming lies you've believed requires a revelation from God that changes your thinking, engages your emotions, and produces sustainable change in your behaviors.
>
> Have you ever received a revelation directly from God? Describe.

4. WHAT LIES DO TO YOU

a. Lies increase your fear.

God wants you to be cautious of things that can hurt you, such as jumping off a cliff, but He doesn't want you to fear the things that His Word says you can overcome. Even though Philippians 4:13 says, "I can do all things through Him who strengthens me," you may find "all things" hard to accept. Why? The lies you've believed have affected you so deeply they've erected emotional bondage to fear in you. Lies handcuff your life experiences and cause you to cower in fear and unbelief.

b. Lies limit your usefulness to God.

If the enemy can bind you with fear, he limits your usefulness to God. For example, if you've ever flubbed your lines in a play, you may have been so humiliated you never again spoke in front of people. As a result, you can't lead a Bible study or perhaps even facilitate a group discussion. Rather than believing God can empower you to do anything, you succumb to fear created by a lie.

c. Lies hinder your fellowship with others.

When you feel rejected, the onset of fear can paralyze you by telling you that others don't like you and you shouldn't share your life with them. These lies tell you that it's better to be alone. Lies steal community and fellowship with other believers and lead to isolation.

d. Lies make you believe God has not forgiven and cleansed your sin.

The devil's biggest lie is that you have not been cleansed from your sins through the blood of Jesus by His death on the cross. The devil also says you don't deserve forgiveness. These lies create shame and make you hide and keep secrets. You become just like Adam and Eve, hiding from God in shame. But God wants you to embrace His forgiveness that enables you to be open, broken, and free.

Sometimes the enemy may say you just need to "forgive yourself"—a popular thought, even among Christians. But forgiving yourself is not in the Bible. All forgiveness comes from God. When you say you need to forgive yourself, you're also saying God's forgiveness isn't sufficient. That's a lie. God's forgiveness is complete, and His forgiveness (not yours) is what you need.

When you truly see and receive God's amazing grace and forgiveness, you no longer believe you need to forgive yourself. Why? Because you know and feel God's complete forgiveness and cleansing.

Instead of saying you need to forgive yourself, tell yourself the truth: I need to understand and fully receive God's forgiveness made available to me through His love, the grace of the Lord Jesus, and the fellowship of the Holy Spirit. Then you can let yourself off the hook and stop your penance. He paid the full price for your forgiveness.

Key Thought:

Lies are woven into the things you **fear** and place **limits** on your life.

How have the lies that you've believed limited your life?

5. HOW TO OVERCOME LIES

a. Name the lie.

When you believe a lie, you don't know you've received a lie because you're immersed in deception and can't rely on your natural wisdom to identify the lie. Therefore, you must rely on the Holy Spirit to lead you into all truth.

Of course, for the Holy Spirit to lead you, you must be willing for Him to search your heart and mind and reveal the lie. Then you can name the lie for what it is—a lie.

> Search me, God, and know my heart; Put me to the test and know my anxious thoughts; And see if there is any hurtful way in me, and lead me in the everlasting way. (Ps. 139:23–24)

Identifying lies starts with being open to the Holy Spirit, who reveals lies to you, and realizing you're reliant on Him to lead you into truth. Reliance on your natural abilities holds your heart and mind in the position to be deceived easily by the enemy.

Key Thought:

Ask the Holy Spirit to help you **identify** what lies you have believed.

What are they?

b. Discover the birth of the lie.

Ask the Holy Spirit to take you backward in your life to discover your first memory of a lie you believed. All lies start somewhere. You may need to think back to your childhood, a parent, a teacher, or someone else. Figuring out where a lie began will help you realize it was just a lie!

> 🔑 **Key Thought:**
>
> What is your **first memory** of this lie? What did you see, hear, or experience? Was it an intruding thought?

c. Confess your collaboration.

Once you discover where a lie started, ask the Holy Spirit to show you when your thinking changed. In other words, when did you agree with the lie spoken over you?

> 🔑 **Key Thought:**
>
> Acknowledge that you entered into a conversation with the enemy about the lie, shook hands with him, and **agreed** with him about the lie. Describe the agreement you made.

d. Admit your responsibility.

Confess to God that you collaborated with the devil by receiving the lie, even when you heard what God had spoken over your life. Always bear in mind that the devil is seeking to devour by speaking lies, destruction, and death over your life, but God speaks truth, health, and life.

> 🔑 **Key Thought:**
>
> Take **responsibility** for your conversation with the enemy and ask God's forgiveness.

e. Renounce the lie.

Replacing truth with a lie is not just a mental acknowledgment. It's a spiritual battle because the enemy designed the lie to destroy you in every regard. Therefore, ask God to break the lie and its impact on your life.

Begin speaking the truth out loud: "I do not believe the lie anymore. I am resting in God's truth."

> ### 🗝 Key Thought:
>
> Ask God to **break** the lie in Jesus's name, help you to believe His truth, and take back the ground you surrendered to the enemy.

f. Confess the lie to others.

Lies thrive in secrecy. Letting others know you believed lies and are now choosing to believe the truth (because you now see the truth) puts you on the path to healing. Even though you may not feel healed yet, confess the lie to others, knowing you trust God to manifest your healing over time.

> ### 🗝 Key Thought:
>
> Confess to others the **lies** you've believed to embrace your healing.

g. Meditate on God's truth.

> Therefore, if you have been raised with Christ, keep seeking the things that are above, where Christ is, seated at the right hand of God. Set your minds on the things that are above, not on the things that are on earth. (Col. 3:1–2)

> For the mind set on the flesh is death, but the mind set on the Spirit is life and peace. (Rom. 8:6)

> You [God] will keep in perfect peace all who trust in you, all whose thoughts are fixed on you! (Isa. 26:3, NLT)

> Watch over your heart with all diligence, for from it flow the springs of life. (Prov. 4:23)

Your mind naturally wants to rest on something. You can't make your mind totally blank. So, you must daily "set your mind on the things that are above, not on the things that are on earth."

Set your mind purposefully on truth each day through time spent with God, reading His Word and talking with Him in prayer. Many people set aside time in the mornings, wanting the help of God's truth throughout the day, to discern what's happening around them and help guard their thoughts against the world's tug.

If you're unaccustomed to spending time with God each day, a great Bible reading plan is the "Daily Audio Bible" at www.dailyaudiobible.com. The app provides a daily reading and listening plan, and the commentary that Brian Hardin adds each day is insightful. Give it a try! We've heard a lot of testimonies that the Word of God through this app has changed lives!

🔑 Key Thought:

Take steps to allow your **mind** to rest on God's **truth** through each day, rather than the enemy's **lies**.

Is there a lie that you would like to have prayer for to release its effect on your life?

After the group session, turn to Appendix A and complete the Two-Minute Takeaway.

Session 3: Homework Assignment

IMPACT OF GENERATIONAL BELIEFS AND VALUES

Our family lineages have the most impact on our lives of any group of people. Their beliefs, values, and actions impact us in ways we may not fully realize, and we pass these down to our children and future generations without much thought.

God wants us to take personal responsibility for lies passed to us from our families of origin and be free from everything that keeps us from believing His truth.

1. On the following template:

    a. Checkmark the lies you believe(d) that were prompted by particular family members.
    b. Follow the directions listed in the right-hand column.
    c. Don't accept being a victim!

Generational Messages about Beliefs and Values — The Lies	Checkmark Source of Message — Parents	Grand-parents	Other Family	Describe how the lies impacted your life and marriage by: 1. asking God to reveal who you have become due to the soil you were planted in, and how you can take personal responsibility; and 2. asking God and your spouse to show you what these family messages are doing in your own family.
MONEY				
Money is the best source of security.				
Money makes you important.				
Making lots of money proves you "made it."				
Money is the key to happiness.				
You should be poor to be godly.				
Giving to others is not a priority.				
Flaunt your wealth and generosity.				

CONFLICT			
Avoid conflict at all costs.			
Better to stuff feelings than make people mad.			
Loud, angry, constant fighting is normal.			
Wait for the other person to say they're sorry.			
Isolation is a good way to deal with conflict.			
SEX			
Sex is not to be spoken about openly.			
Men can be promiscuous; women must be chaste.			
Sexuality in marriage will come easily.			
Sex is dirty.			
Sex is a physical need.			
Using pornography is acceptable.			
Using pornography will enhance our sex life.			
Masturbation is a good way to satisfy sexual needs.			
It's okay to be gay/lesbian.			
Women should serve men sexually.			
GRIEF AND LOSS			
Sadness is a sign of weakness.			
You are not allowed to be depressed.			
Get over losses quickly, and move on.			
Don't cry.			

EXPRESSING ANGER			
Anger is bad and dangerous.			
Explode in anger to make a point.			
Sarcasm is an acceptable way to release anger.			
Using profanity is normal.			
Hitting or other physical abuse is normal.			
FAMILY			
You owe your parents for all they've done for you.			
You should bury your family's "dirty laundry."			
Duty to family comes before everything.			
Your mother and father come before your spouse.			
Making your spouse the butt of your jokes is okay.			
Criticizing your spouse is acceptable.			
Throwing your spouse "under the bus" is acceptable.			
RELATIONSHIPS			
Don't trust people; they will let you down.			
Ignore hurt to reconcile relationships.			
Don't show vulnerability.			
Intimate relationships with the opposite sex other than your spouse are okay.			
You don't need any friends.			

CULTURAL ATTITUDES			
Only choose friends who are like you.			
Do not marry someone of a different culture or race.			
Certain cultures and races are not as good as your own.			
SUCCESS			
Success is getting into the best schools.			
Success is making lots of money and having things.			
Success is getting married and having children.			
Success is a prestigious job.			
Success is earning degrees, titles, or certifications.			
Success defines your worth and what people think of you.			
FEELINGS/EMOTIONS			
You are not allowed to show certain feelings.			
Your feelings are not important.			
Reacting without thinking is okay.			
Showing emotions is a sign of weakness.			
Alcohol and drugs are normal ways to manage or fix emotional pain.			
You are genetically not emotional.			

SESSION 3: OVERCOMING THE LIES OF THE ENEMY

MARRIAGE			
Divorce is an option.			
Fornication has minimal impact.			
Adultery can be ignored or tolerated.			
Abuse can be hidden and tolerated.			
Weaknesses should be hidden from children.			
Only superficial communication is normal.			
Affection should not be seen openly.			

2. Identify and record the **five most significant lies** from the completed worksheet above. Follow the prompts in these columns:

Describe the five most significant lies.	How did the lie start? What is your earliest memory? Ask God for a revelation.
1.	
2.	
3.	
4.	
5.	

SESSION 3: OVERCOMING THE LIES OF THE ENEMY

3. With your spouse:

   a. Review the Impact of Generational Beliefs and Values worksheet in Question 1 above.
   b. Review your answers to Question 2 above.
   c. Share about each lie you believe(d), using the following prompts:
      - What is the true pain or hurt in how the lie has affected you?
      - How has the lie caused you to manage your image?
      - What secrets has the lie caused you to keep from your spouse and others?
      - Accept personal responsibility for conversations you had or agreements with the devil about the lie and your continued belief in the lie.
      - Ask your spouse what impact the lie has had on them and how the impact has made them feel.
      - Apologize to your spouse for each negative impact and how it has made them feel.
      - Forgive, bless, and pray for the individual who spoke the lie to or about you. Example: Child heard his dad tell his mom, "He's a stupid kid who won't amount to anything."
      - Work with your spouse to identify a Bible verse that replaces the lie with truth.
   d. Pray together, renouncing each lie you believed. Feel free to use the following prayer as an example:

   God, thank You for revealing to me through the Holy Spirit that I was deceived into believing that [name the lie; describe its impact]. I was responsible for believing this lie and for the way this lie affected me and [name people the lie affected].

   Thank You that I am now standing in the truth of Your promises, specifically, [name God's promise in the Bible]. I will no longer be under the power of this lie. I declare that I am free from this day forward, and I'm trusting the Holy Spirit to enable me to stand in God's truth. Thank You for setting me free! Amen!

4. With your spouse, share your Two-Minute Takeaway from Session 3. Record their observations and your agreed-upon action steps.

Notes

SESSION 4:
THE SAVAGE HELPER

Excerpt from *Savage Marriage*

Phil

Although the emotional pain I'd experienced on the plane home had been monstrous, it was nothing like the agony of confessing to my wife and witnessing the visceral effects in her.

On the plane, I could only imagine Priscilla's reaction. In the reality of our kitchen, she was ablaze with anguish, anger, disgust, and despair, painting a horrendous picture of what my sin had done to her heart. Her every move, tear, and word dripped with fury from my betrayal, paralyzing me as our tears flowed uncontrollably under the tormenting weight of my sin.

When the pace of her questions had slowed, we sat in lifeless silence. Neither of us knew what more to say.

She now knew everything, which made clear to her why there had been distance between us for so many years, why I had for so long disconnected from her emotionally, and why she had angry dreams of betrayal.

There had always been a secret life embedded in our marriage that I'd worked hard to keep hidden, desperate to protect Priscilla (and me) from pain.

The consuming pain she was now under held no hope that our reality would get easier. Clearly, I had a seriously destructive problem in my brain. *God, is Priscilla part of Your plan to help me overcome and heal?*

I thought back to Paul Speed's words: "When you don't know what to do next, humility is always the answer." I knew I needed to take another step deeper into authentic humility. I pointed to my head and, in desperation, pleaded, "Priscilla, I am *so* sick. My mind is broken! I need your help to get it fixed. Will you help me?"

Priscilla

Phil's words were soft, contemplative, and humble, reflecting a brokenness I'd never seen in him. Although his request was simple, it was a profound switch in his attitude toward me. He had never asked for my help with anything, except chores related to the kids, our home, and making him look better. He had always been self-assured and in charge. It was unnerving to see him bent over in weakness, needing something only I could provide. But my emotions were still raging, making me want to exact vengeance rather than provide help. *Hell no! After what you've done, you're on your own.*

But still, his quiet plea, "Will you help me?" got my attention, and his typical arrogance was replaced with a brokenness and contriteness I'd never witnessed in him. He looked so lost. His shoulders were slumped in defeat, his head was bowed, and his red eyes begged, *Please help me; I can't do this alone.*

As I further pondered his appeal, in sight of his radical loss of pride—a man I barely recognized—a tiny feeling of mercy, a sliver of compassion, opened my heart. *Phil is my husband. We've been married for longer than I've lived without him, and he's the father of our five children.*

Still enraged and a slave to my broken heart, I guardedly agreed to at least help him find healing. I couldn't promise more than that. "Okay, we'll get through this. I'll help you get fixed."

1. THE NEED FOR COMPANIONSHIP

This is the account of the heavens and the earth when they were created, in the day that the Lord God made earth and heaven. . . . Then the Lord God formed the man of dust from the ground, and breathed into his nostrils the breath of life; and the man became a living person. The Lord God planted a garden toward the east, in Eden; and there He placed the man whom He had formed. . . . Then the Lord God took the man and put him in the Garden of Eden to cultivate it and tend it. . . . Then the Lord God said, "It is not good for the man to be alone; I will make him a helper suitable for him." . . . So the Lord God caused a deep sleep to fall upon the man, and he slept; then He took one of his ribs and closed up the flesh at that place. And the Lord God fashioned into a woman the rib which He had taken from the man, and brought her to the man. (Gen. 2:4–22)

Have you ever wondered why God said it wasn't good for Adam to be alone, although Adam wasn't alone?

Look closely at the Scripture. Adam was with God! It's inconceivable to think Adam needed anyone else when he walked and talked with God every day! So why did God say it wasn't good for man to be alone?

God wasn't making an observation about Adam's condition. He was declaring His purposeful design for man. God hadn't made an oversight, and He didn't look at Adam and say, "Whoops, I made a mistake. I thought everything I made was good, but now I realize I missed something!"

"It's not good for man to be alone" was God's first declaration about His intended design and condition of man. Creating a human being who would need to dwell in unity with other human beings was part of His plan for the world.

Why is this factor important?

His plan showed that His first purpose for Eve's creation was human companionship for Adam.

Some people believe that procreation was the reason for Eve's existence. But God had already brought two people into existence without a physical birth, and He certainly could have created more. Notice it wasn't until after the fall of man (the sin of eating the forbidden fruit) that God said Eve would give birth to other human beings.

Others believe Adam needed a woman because he couldn't control his sexual appetite. But it wasn't until after Adam saw Eve that his sexuality became real to him.

So, the first and main reason for Eve's existence was companionship.

But wasn't God a sufficient companion for Adam? Why would Adam need someone else?

God was looking into the future, knowing Adam would sin and that the sin would be an unholy wedge in their relationship, separating Adam from his holy God. (Read Hab. 1:13 and Matt. 27:45–46.) God would send Adam out of the Garden of Eden in that fallen state (Gen. 3:23).

For the first time, Adam would feel alone. He would be not only physically alone but spiritually alone, away from the presence of God. Adam would long to be reunited with God, but his best human efforts to seek God would be futile. Adam's loneliness would overwhelm him spiritually and emotionally. God knew Adam's future and provided Eve (before the fall) to help Adam in his pursuit of God (after the fall). God's purpose for Eve's existence was first spiritual, followed by emotional, and then sexual.

Companionship isn't accomplished merely by living together. Many people live together but still feel alone because they aren't experiencing true intimacy. God's companionship purpose for couples is reflected in their spiritual, emotional, and sexual intimacy. This complete threefold intimacy makes loneliness flee!

Key Thought:

Companionship isn't about **proximity**. It's about **spiritual**, **emotional**, and **physical** intimacy that cures loneliness and helps each spouse pursue God's purpose and plan for their life.

When have you felt spiritually, emotionally, or sexually alone in your marriage?

2. HUSBANDS NEED TO EMBRACE THEIR HELPER

Ever hear jokes about husbands never asking for directions, even though their wives may know the route? The jokes point to an underlying truth: men don't like to ask for help!

God knew this would be a big problem, so He made this very clear to Adam: "You need a helper!" Most men don't realize what type of help they need, and they erroneously conclude that their help comes from anyone except their wives!

Let's look at God's design for Eve as Adam's helper. God created Adam out of nonliving material (dust) but constructed (not created) Eve from Adam's living flesh. God breathed into Adam's nostrils His own breath of life—but God didn't breathe into Eve's nostrils. So where did her living breath come from? Her life came from Adam's, whose life had come from God.

God had not needed to breathe into Eve's nostrils, just as He doesn't need to breathe into newborn infants, as their physical breath is part of the regeneration of life from their mothers and fathers.

Do you see how it made complete sense for Adam to love Eve? He saw her as part of his own body because she had come out of him. Adam's thought of being "one flesh" with Eve wasn't a lofty goal but a concluded fact. Likewise, God wants husbands to love their wives in that powerful way.

Husbands: To love your wife as God intended, you must see her through the same God-given spiritual eyes that Adam saw Eve. When you embrace your wife as part of yourself—one flesh—and treat her as your divine, God-given helper, she will sense her God-given purpose in the relationship. Anything short of seeing your wife as Adam saw Eve is contrived and ultimately not spiritually satisfying.

Satan knows the God-vested power of wives as helpers in marriage relationships, and he uses deception to break the unity between spouses. When marriages become difficult, spouses hear the same lie: "You'd be better off by yourself." While this may at times be the right course (situations of abuse), it's not the right path for the vast majority of conflicts.

Satan whispers that deadly lie in our ears to confront God's Word, knowing that when "a house is divided against itself, that house will not be able to stand" (Mark 3:25).

Consider from the following passage what happened after Adam and Eve sinned (eating the forbidden fruit).

> Now they heard the sound of the Lord God walking in the garden in the cool of the day, and the man and his wife hid themselves from the presence of the Lord God among the trees of the garden. Then the Lord God called to the man, and said to him, "Where are you?" He said, "I heard the sound of You in the garden, and I was afraid because I was naked; so I hid myself." And He said, "Who told you that you were naked? Have you eaten from the tree from which I commanded you not to eat?" The man said, "The woman whom You gave to be with me, she gave me some of the fruit of the tree, and I ate." (Gen. 3:8–12)

The serpent spoke a lie right after they sinned. He was trying to create unbelief in Adam about God's word that Eve was a suitable helper. Believing the lie, Adam went into a downward spiral and turned against Eve (whom he had prior declared was bone of his bone and flesh of his flesh, and with whom he was sexually intimate), blaming her for his sin. Adam had agreed with a lie planted by the serpent: *Eve isn't a suitable helper at all! She's actually the source of your first big problem!*

The same lie continues to be spoken by the enemy into husbands' ears, and they often conclude their wives are not their helpers. They agree with Satan that their wives are the source of all their problems. The whole world has bought into this lie and acts on it, unaware the enemy has played them.

Have you ever noticed that when you hear the name Eve, the first thing that likely pops into your mind is a picture of Eve handing an apple to Adam? For ages, Eve has been portrayed and seen as the villain.

Our warped thinking is the real issue in marriages.

With the mindset that wives are the villains, how can we believe that Eve was God's complete solution for Adam's need for help? If she wasn't God's solution, shouldn't God have made somebody else, maybe "Jack," Adam's accountability partner? And what about the counselor Adam would need to work through his communication problems with Eve? And what about Adam's need for golfing buddies?

While there's nothing wrong with acquiring the help of counselors and fellow brothers, if what Adam had needed to solve his problem was another man, God did Adam a disservice by creating a woman, a wife.

Husbands and wives: When any roles outside your marriage relationship begin to take the place of your spousal relationship, you are not experiencing God's best, His ideal solution for husbands and wives that He intended from the beginning. Men's groups, women's groups, counselors, and accountability partners sometimes encourage confession within that setting but allow spouses to keep secrets from each other. Secrets kept by either husband or wife destroy the "suitable" relationship God intended.

The phrase *suitable helper* is very interesting. Only one time in the Bible are the two words combined. *Suitable helper* is sometimes translated from Hebrew as "helpmeet" and has been the subject of much debate and error regarding the role of the wife. So what is the role of wives?

Man is made in God's image and reflects God's glory. And woman reflects man's glory. (1 Cor. 11:7, NLT)

Adam, created first, directly reflected God's image. Eve reflected God's image because she was created through Adam, and as a result, she also reflected Adam's image or glory. Eve was a type of barometer of Adam, sort of like a mirror. The wife's countenance mirrors what is happening inside her husband. When you see a wife doing great, you'll likely conclude that her husband is also doing great. The glory of the husband is reflected in the wife. Conversely, if a wife is depressed, anxious, fearful, or discouraged, her husband is commonly not doing well.

The implication is that if you want to see how a husband is doing with God, look at his wife's countenance, for she will reflect her husband's relationship with Christ as her husband's "helpmeet."

The Genesis 2:18 description, *helper suitable,* is translated from the Hebrew terms *ezer*, meaning "a help; helper,"[1] and *kenegdo. The root word of kenegdo is neged,* meaning "in front of, in sight of, opposite to."[2]

In other words, the *suitable helper* is someone very close to and directly in front of man (like a mirror), helping him see his opposite view. For example, the wife helps the husband see where he's making mistakes and what he may be missing or neglecting in his thoughts, feelings, and behaviors.

Ezer is a word with an interesting derivation and deep meaning. In "The Real Meaning of the Term 'Help Meet,'" Heather Farrell quoted:

> According to biblical scholar David Freedman, the Hebrew word translated into English as "help" is ezer. This word is a combination of two roots, one meaning "to rescue," "to save," and the other meaning "to be strong." Just as the roots merged into one word, so did their meanings. At first ezer meant either "to save" or "to be strong," but in time, said Freedman, ezer "was always interpreted as 'to help,' a mixture of both nuances."
>
> The noun ezer occurs 21 times in the Hebrew Bible. In eight of these instances the word means "savior." These examples are easy to identify because they are associated with other expressions of deliverance or saving. Elsewhere in the Bible, the root ezer means "strength."[3]

The places where ezer is used most often refers to how God was an ezer to Israel.

An example is the following passage from Exodus. God was going to kill Moses for not circumcising his son, and his wife, Zipporah, came to his aid.

---

1 Bible Hub, s.v. "ezer," accessed March 18, 2022, https://biblehub.com/hebrew/5828.htm.
2 Bible Hub, s.v. "Kenegdo," accessed March 18, 2022, https://biblehub.com/hebrew/5048.htm.
3 Heather Farrell, "The Real Meaning of the Term 'Help Meet,'" Women in the Scriptures, https://www.womeninthescriptures.com/2010/11/real-meaning-of-term-help-meet.html

> It came about at the overnight encampment on the way, that the Lord met Moses, and sought to put him to death. So Zipporah took a flint and cut off her son's foreskin and threw it at Moses' feet; and she said, "You are indeed a groom of blood to me." So He left him alone. At that time she said, "You are a groom of blood"—because of the circumcision. (Ex. 4:24–26)

Do you see what happened? Zipporah came to Moses's rescue by grabbing a flint knife and circumcising their son. Now that's a Savage Helper!

God empowered women to help and even rescue their husbands, but regrettably, many men easily or quickly reject their wives and blame them for their own mistakes (like Adam did with Eve). They blame their wives for everything wrong, seeing their wives as the problem instead of the solution.

Simply by observing men and women, we see the mirror effect. Have you noticed that men and women seem almost opposite in their natural strengths and tendencies? Consider these generalizations:

- The man may show physical strength, whereas the woman may be physically weaker.
- The man may be less verbal and task-oriented and the woman more verbal and relationship-oriented.
- The man may tend to think logically and the woman abstractly.

God designed man and woman to shore up each other's weaknesses. A wife intuitively senses what's going on inside her husband and can uniquely come to his spiritual aid when he needs help. Together, husband and wife are stronger, mutually capable of helping each other meet their spirit's, soul's, and body's needs. They help each other be complete—as one—not alone in their respective thoughts, tendencies, and weaknesses.

Now we have the exceptional picture of why Eve was described as a *kenegdo ezer* or "helpmeet." Eve would be like a mirror directly in front of Adam, reflecting who he was and providing strength to help rescue him, similar to how God rescued us! Wow! That's a Savage Helper! This picture of man and woman as husband and wife is very different from how men, society, and our religious institutions have portrayed the role of wives.

🔑 Key Thought:

Wives are designed to **reflect** their husband's relationship with God.

How have you seen this principle at work in your marriage?

3. WIVES ARE LIFE-GIVERS

The common picture of Eve standing beside Adam, giving him an apple, is how society has portrayed women: she's a problem, and a man needs to lead and direct her so she doesn't become more of a problem.

However, that wasn't her God-given nature. God designed and saw the woman as a life-giver, and Adam named her accordingly—*Eve* means "mother of all *the* living" (Gen. 3:20).

While it's certainly true that women are the givers of physical life through their ability to give birth, women are also designed to be givers of emotional life.

Have you noticed how much more relational women typically are than men? How women generally use words more? How they more naturally demonstrate feelings? Women's ability to relate emotionally gives life—enjoyment and other positive feelings—to our souls. We see this exuberant life displayed between many moms and their children. Mom is often the first caregiver to be called by her children, and she responds with caring words and expressions of interest, exuding and encouraging confidence. Her children confide in her because she gives emotional life to them.

Key Thought:

Wives are designed to be **life-givers**.

How have you seen this in your marriage, or how would you like to see this in your marriage?

4. WIVES ARE STRONG

> You husbands in the same way, live with your wives in an understanding way, as with someone weaker, since she is a woman; and show her honor as a fellow heir of the grace of life, so that your prayers will not be hindered. (1 Peter 3:7)

Some have interpreted this often-quoted verse to mean that wives are weak in every way and husbands need to help them. Notice this is precisely the opposite of how God made Adam and Eve. He said Adam needed help. And if Adam needed help, don't you think God would have given him someone strong and able as his helper?

In truth, *weaker* in 1 Peter 3:7 means physically weaker. In some Bible translations, the phrase *weaker vessel* appears—*vessel* meaning woman. When considering God's intention, it's important to note that *vessel* indicates that men are to treat their wives with great tenderness and care, as they would treat fine, delicate crystal.

Though women are physically weaker, God created women spiritually and emotionally strong, a helper able to be a helper! He designed the woman to help the man with all his weaknesses and gave the woman grace to deal with man's weaknesses. Women are strong!

> **🔑 Key Thought:**
>
> Wives were built by God to be **strong**.
>
> Describe a situation where you have observed the emotional and spiritual strength of women.

5. THE CYCLE OF LOVE AND RESPECT

> Husbands, love your wives, just as Christ also loved the church and gave Himself up for her. (Eph. 5:25)

In this verse, the Greek word used for "love" is *agapaó*[4] (often heard as *agape*), and refers to unconditional, self-sacrificing love. Sometimes *agape* is described as the type of love God showed by sending His son to die for us: unconditional love not requiring us to earn it.

What does this mean about the husband's agape love toward his wife? The husband's love should be unconditional, requiring nothing of her in return. He should love his wife even when she appears unlovable because that is the love God demonstrated toward us.

If the husband is supposed to love his wife unconditionally, what is the wife supposed to do? We see the answer a few verses later in Ephesians.

> Each husband is to love his own wife the same as himself; and the wife must see to it that she respects her husband. (Eph. 5:33)

God commanded wives to respect their husbands instead of a command to love them. Does this mean she should respect him unconditionally like he is supposed to love her unconditionally?

While people agree that love should be unconditional, many believe respect should be earned. However, Ephesians 5:33 does not say that. God presented respect as something the wife should "see to it" that she does. Just like the husband should demonstrate unconditional love, the wife should show unconditional respect.

> In the same way, you wives, be subject to your own husbands so that even if any of them are disobedient to the word, they may be won over without a word by the behavior of their wives, as they observe your pure and respectful behavior. (1 Peter 3:1–2)

Even when wives live with unbelieving husbands, they can win them over to Christ by their respectful behavior. Many wives would say there is very little to respect in an unbelieving husband. But that stance doesn't change Scripture, which says the wife is to behave respectfully toward her husband, indicating the husband does not earn her respect.

---

4 Bible Hub, s.v. "agapaó," accessed March 18, 2022, https://biblehub.com/greek/25.htm.

The wife longs for security in her husband's love, and the husband longs to be respected by his wife. The unconditional love and respect required by God meet the husband's and wife's greatest needs.

God's commands do not mean the wife shouldn't love her husband and the husband shouldn't respect his wife but that we recognize that God endowed agape love into the natural creation of the woman, which is readily evident in the way she treats her family. Ever notice who willingly makes sure the whole family has enough to eat first? Who takes the smallest piece of pie? Who self-sacrifices her time to care for the needs of the children? Yes, the wife.

What about the husband?

God created the husband with a role of honor and valor for his family. When a boat is sinking, everyone yells, "Women and children first." Men go to war and will take a bullet to save their families. So innately, men desire the respect that goes to someone willing to die.

Often marriage becomes stuck because the wife is waiting for her husband's love to show her respect, and the husband is waiting for her respect to show his love. When neither spouse moves, isolation and silence set in. In Dr. Emerson Eggerichs' book *Love & Respect*, he calls this the "crazy cycle." (We highly recommend the book. We adopted many concepts in this section from *Love & Respect*.)

The point of love and respect follows the law of sowing and reaping. When husbands sow love into their wives by giving up their lives, their wives reap respect. Likewise, when wives sow respect into their husbands, they reap their husbands' love.

This propagation of love and respect was evident in the garden. Consider what Adam said when he saw Eve for the first time: "Bone of my bones, and flesh of my flesh" (Gen. 2:23). His words and actions demonstrated love for her immediately, thereby unearned.

But have you ever wondered how Eve reacted?

The Bible doesn't answer this question, but some people believe that Eve's knowledge of being made from elements inside Adam created respect in her for him because he had submitted part of himself for her (though God did the giving). So you can see, even in their first meeting, the love and respect cycle.

> Older women likewise are to be reverent in their behavior, not malicious gossips nor enslaved to much wine, teaching what is good, so that they may encourage the young women to love their husbands, to love their children. (Titus 2:3–4)

Women are also encouraged to love their husbands, but this verse uses a different Greek word for love—*phileó*,[5] which means a brotherly or friendly type of love. Phileó addresses kindness, respect, and not having a scowl when arguing. Even though wives naturally demonstrate agape (self-sacrificing love), showing friendly, brotherly type love can sometimes present a challenge. In arguments, women are more naturally pulled in emotionally and sometimes react with unkind frustration (as can men).

When a husband feels his wife's unkindness, he may interpret that as a lack of respect and frequently respond with a lack of love. Thereby, while wives tend to have fewer challenges with agape love, they sometimes have challenges with phileó love, which is the point of the verse and why God instructs the older women to teach younger women how to love their husbands and children in a phileó manner.

---

[5] Bible Hub, s.v. "Phileó," accessed March 18, 2022, https://biblehub.com/greek/5368.htm.

> *Husbands, lack of respect from your wife is no excuse for not loving her; and wives, a lack of love from your husband is no excuse for not respecting him.*

Wives and husbands, when your spouse doesn't show you love or respect and you use their behavior as an excuse to withhold love or respect, the crazy cycle ensues. One of you must break the cycle, and it should be the one who sees themselves as the most spiritually mature. Meaning either the husband must demonstrate his love regardless of the situation, or the wife must demonstrate her respect.

If neither of you makes a move, your relationship will remain stuck in the crazy cycle. In the face of not feeling loved, no one wants to show respect, and no one wants to show love in the face of not feeling respected.

The key is humility.

Only the humble spouse will be able to move past their feelings and show unconditional love and unconditional respect. When one spouse humbles themselves, they are empowered to break the crazy cycle.

Key Thought:

Husbands must **love** their wives unconditionally, and wives must **respect** their husbands unconditionally.

How has the crazy cycle affected your marriage?

6. FOUR MALE PREJUDICES

(The following was adapted from *Discovering the Mind of a Woman* by Ken Nair):

a. Myth 1: Women are impossible to understand.

> You husbands in the same way, live with your wives in an understanding way. (1 Peter 3:7)

Even though God commanded husbands to understand their wives, this is the subject of many jokes, implying that women can't be understood—so many men don't even try. Worsening the mindset is some saying women can't even understand themselves.

In a certain sense, women's minds are more complex than men's. For example, women can juggle thoughts and activities much better than men, particularly emotions. In that regard, husbands often don't understand what's going on inside their wives. Husbands then grow frustrated and give up. Then they decide to separate themselves emotionally and interactively, preferring to not get in the way of their wives seemingly "living in their own worlds."

Myth Buster:

Instead, a husband needs to be a student of his wife with the help of the Holy Spirit. He should ask his wife questions toward understanding her complex thought processes and feelings.

God knows women intimately as Creator, and the Holy Spirit can help husbands understand them. As intuitive, deep-thinking women, wives want to know and understand their husbands. Continually pursuing to know each other creates confidence in women that they are loved and fuels their desire to know and respect their husbands.

b. Myth 2: Women are the real problem.

Remember that just after Adam sinned, he complained to God that Eve had given him the forbidden fruit, citing her as the real problem. Many husbands don't see their wives as the solution but as part or all of the marriage problems. This mindset is directly contrary to what God intended for men.

Rather than taking responsibility for marital problems, many husbands first point out to their wives that they were also partially responsible.

Even when men confess their sins to their wives, many husbands will blame their sins on their wives. For example, if he was unfaithful, he may tell his wife it's because she wasn't providing enough sex. When he says he wasn't always truthful, he may say it's because she gets upset when he tells her the truth.

Men also sometimes see their wives as a vending machine—he puts in a house, car, clothes, food, and perhaps a date night and gifts and believes he's thereby entitled to get something in return, which is principally sex, although he also enjoys the clean house and good food. So, when his wife complains that he doesn't care about her, he says, "Hey, what about everything I provide for you?"

Myth Buster:

What a wife really wants from her husband is a broken, humble companion who pursues to know her heart and demonstrates that he authentically cares about her feelings.

When a wife doesn't sense and see these from her husband, she may numb her pain by looking for something that feels like a void filler—such as new cars, clothes, alcohol, drugs, and even other relationships. However, most women would trade all such things for a man who demonstrates he truly loves and cares for her.

To effectively meet his wife's needs, a husband must learn to *understand* his wife and her needs. That can be hard, but adopting and practicing the truths in this session and throughout this study will enable you to know and understand your wife better.

First, grasp that when you become frustrated trying to understand your wife's feelings and thinking, you can start thinking and believing the myth that she is to blame for all your problems. Recognize, right away, that this is a lie from the enemy to destroy your relationship.

When you buy into the lie, conversations with your wife may stir up impatience, criticism, and accusations, which quickly kill emotional intimacy, making it impossible for you and your wife to experience real joy and oneness.

c. Myth 3: Women are inferior to men.

Men who see their wives as inferior tend to treat their wives like servants. The husband believes God gave him a "helper" to take care of his needs, including everything to do with the family and home while he's free to chase his dreams.

Believing your wife is inferior will also show up in communication with her. Have you ever heard your wife say, "You make me feel stupid"? The answer for many men is yes. They doubt their wives' opinions, they don't take their wives' thoughts seriously, and thereby they don't take their wives' advice. They will ask others for solutions before they ask their wives, and they will do and say other things that make their wives feel inferior.

When a wife senses and feels that her husband regards her as inferior, she develops a poor self-image, lacks confidence, and second-guesses herself. And because she feels inferior, she doesn't confront her husband's pride.

Myth Buster:

Your wife needs to hear these truths from you: she is intelligent, capable, intuitive, spiritual, and needed.

Your wife wants to see your humility that invites and embraces her advice, reproof, ideas, and insights.

Men need to see that women are not inferior; they are very strong mentally, emotionally, and spiritually.

At the time of Jesus's crucifixion, all His disciples fled from Him. But the women who had followed Him were with Him at His crucifixion (Mark 15:40–42) and His tomb. The women were the first to see Jesus resurrected and the ones who first told others that He was alive (Mark 16).

The women were the strong ones! Your wife is strong.

d. Myth 4: Men are always supposed to be the boss.

Because men may conclude that their wives are the real problem and are inferior to men, some husbands believe they should naturally be the bosses. This lie has led (and continues to lead) many men to dominate women and place them in a subservient role.

1 Corinthians 11:3 speaks of God as the head of Christ, Christ as the head of man, and man as the head of woman, which means order of authority—not bossing. When a husband fulfills God's command to dwell in unity with Him, the man is then empowered to work toward and embrace common decision-making with his wife, and the couple will look out for each other's needs more than their own.

> Do nothing from selfishness or empty conceit, but with humility of mind consider one another as more important than yourselves. (Phil. 2:3)

Myth Buster:

Even though Christ is head, God calls His children (male and female) *friends*, not slaves. He said and demonstrated that He wants our marriage relationships to be friendships, with every decision of the husband representing a dying to himself to nurture life in his wife as Jesus did for us. He died so we could have life "and have it abundantly" (John 10:10).

Occasionally, when there's an impasse, someone in the family has to make the hard decision. That falls to the husband. However, his leadership should mirror the way Jesus led: as a servant leader of humility.

The husband shouldn't lord this over his wife but rather embrace the truth of Galatians 3:28: in Christ, everyone is equal.

> There is neither Jew nor Greek, there is neither slave nor free, there is neither male nor female; for you are all one in Christ Jesus. (Gal. 3:28)

The husband who mirrors God's Word and Christ's example will encourage shared husband-and-wife leadership in the family. And he'll remain responsible for every outcome. He will reject passivity and embrace his role as a servant-leader of his family.

🔑 Key Thought:

Both men and women can have **prejudices** about a woman's role.

How have you seen these prejudices in your marriage? What would you like to change?

After the group session, turn to Appendix A and complete your Two-Minute Takeaway.

Session 4: Homework Assignment

Answer the following questions, and then discuss them with your spouse.

1. Describe the example of husband and wife roles you saw in your home growing up. Consider these prompts:

    a. Who was the "head of the house," and how did the other spouse react?
    b. What evidence of love and respect did you see?
    c. Did decision-making reflect an attitude of mutual submission, or was it "my way or the highway"?
    d. Was there evidence of your mother being a Savage Helper, and did your father recognize her as such?
    e. How has your family of origin shaped your current family experience?

2. Discuss your answers above with your spouse. Compare your families of origin and identify how your differing experiences have affected your marriage.

3. Now consider these prompts:

    a. How have your expectations been shaped by what you saw in your family?
    b. What conflicts have those created?
    c. What messages are you sending to your children?
    d. What would you like to change?

4. Discuss your answers above with your spouse and how you can be a better companion to them (spiritually, emotionally, and sexually).

5. Together, review your Two-Minute Takeaway from Session 4, and record action steps.

SESSION 5:
EXPERIENCING SPIRITUAL INTIMACY

Excerpt from *Savage Marriage*

Priscilla

When Phil disclosed his double life to me and our marriage crumbled, there seemed to be nothing left. No matter how well-intentioned we'd been to create emotional intimacy, our efforts hadn't provided the fuel we needed to save our marriage.

Even though magazines and self-help books proclaimed that emotional and sexual intimacy were the keys to a good marriage, they were powerless in the face of real problems.

In the months that followed our repentance from infidelity, apathy, pride, and the like, God showed us what was missing: *spiritual intimacy* with Him and each other.

We had been like many couples; we knew each other emotionally and sexually but not spiritually. If someone had asked me to describe my spiritual relationship with Phil, I would have described our religious activities—going to church, attending and teaching Bible studies, etc. I didn't understand what *spiritual intimacy* meant or looked like as husband and wife.

One morning, I got up extra early and sat beside Phil at the kitchen table. He had been following a daily Bible reading plan since the beginning of the year (four months before coming clean). As I approached and sat down, he said, "I'm reading in First Samuel. Want to join me?"

I found one of the kids' Bibles, opened it to 1 Samuel, and began to read. For the first time in my life, the Word of God came alive to me.

It was remarkable to see God's hand, His graciousness, and His plan for me in Old Testament passages. I had never before had that experience. Unlike my childhood and college days, I was not being forced and was under no obligation to read the Bible; I just wanted to be part of the changes I was witnessing in Phil's life. If the Word of God could change Phil—from a narcissistic, self-centered, prideful know-it-all into someone who shared his feelings and shortcomings and walked in humility before his family and friends—I wanted to experience that supernatural power.

We began reading the Bible every morning. Our time together sometimes stretched into hours of sharing and discussion, and the Word of God became a delight to me. We developed true spiritual intimacy with God and each other as we learned how we each saw God, shared what we were hearing from Him, and recognized how He was changing us and helping us process our grief. Every morning, we gained more healing of our souls, the most beautiful experiences I'd ever had in our marriage.

1. INTIMACY IN SPIRIT, SOUL, AND BODY

> Now may the God of peace Himself sanctify you entirely; and may your spirit and soul and body be kept complete, without blame at the coming of our Lord Jesus Christ. (1 Thess. 5:23)

Christians experience life in Christ through their spirits, souls, and bodies. And in marriage, they should seek intimacy with their spouses in all three parts.

> The Lord God formed the man of dust from the ground, and breathed into his nostrils the breath of life; and the man became a living person. (Gen. 2:7)

Our spirits represent the breath of God that Adam received into his nostrils in the garden. With God's breath, Adam became alive and capable of communicating intimately with God. But when Adam sinned by eating from the tree of the knowledge of good and evil, his spirit died, and God, being holy (sin not a part of His presence), banished Adam and Eve from the garden. (Read Genesis 3.)

> When you were dead in your wrongdoings and the uncircumcision of your flesh, He made you alive together with Him, having forgiven us all our wrongdoings. (Col. 2:13)

When we receive Christ into our lives, our dead spirits are "born again" and once again become alive. At that moment, the Holy Spirit of God enters into us and works with our spirits in that the two are virtually indistinguishable. The Holy Spirit of God communicates with our spirits, which quickens our consciences. We no longer enjoy sinning because our consciences produce guilt and shame for our wrongdoings that prompt us to return to a right relationship (oneness) with God's spirit.

Our souls are our minds, wills, and emotions. The soul is the part of us that makes day-to-day decisions and creates feelings of joy that may prompt laughter and feelings of depression and mourning that may prompt negative reactions. Our emotional gauges reside in our souls and tell us how well or poor our lives and marriages are. When we're joyful, despairing, or numb about our marriages, we feel it in our souls.

We know that our bodies are our physical parts that, when touched, will enact chemical reactions that direct our minds toward actions to satisfy our natural, physical desires. We also know that our bodies house our souls and spirits, and when we die, our bodies will return to dust.

In other words, spiritual, emotional, and physical intimacy are interconnected and interdependent. So, when we don't experience intimacy with our spouses in one of these areas, the other two areas are also negatively affected. For example, when we're emotionally distant from our spouses, it's hard to embrace each other sexually. Likewise, when we aren't connecting sexually in a regular and meaningful way, our emotional relationship suffers.

What about when we're not connecting spiritually with our spouses?

The same thing is true: we don't experience the full blessing of God in our emotional and sexual spousal relationships.

Although many couples who lack spiritual intimacy can connect emotionally and sexually, they don't experience everything God has for them in these areas. They generally settle for less than what's possible—God's best in their emotional and sexual relationships.

Spiritual intimacy between husband and wife is essential to their emotional and physical intimacy. Yet couples often ignore, or are unaware of, spiritual intimacy.

If you're disappointed with your emotional and sexual intimacy, this session will provide a supernatural foundation for change in your relationship.

Key Thought:

In marriage, your spiritual, emotional, and physical intimacy are **interconnected** and **interdependent**.

How have you experienced this connectivity in your marriage?

2. THE ORDER OF INTIMACY

God set the stage for Adam's relationship with Eve to blossom.

> The Lord God said, "It is not good for the man to be alone; I will make him a helper suitable for him." ... So the Lord God caused a deep sleep to fall upon the man, and he slept; then He took one of his ribs and closed up the flesh at that place. And the Lord God fashioned into a woman the rib which He had taken from the man, and brought her to the man. The man said,
>
> "At last this is bone of my bones,
> And flesh of my flesh;
> She shall be called 'woman,'
> Because she was taken out of man."
>
> For this reason a man shall leave his father and his mother, and be joined to his wife; and they shall become one flesh. And the man and his wife were both naked, but they were not ashamed. (Gen. 2:18-25)

Through Adam and Eve's experience, we see God's beautiful plan for men and women to develop spiritual, emotional, and sexual intimacy as husbands and wives.

When Adam woke, his first realization was a spiritual revelation: God had made a being from his flesh—he and Eve were like creations from God. Adam's awakening to Eve was the beginning of their spiritual intimacy together. Both realized their entire purpose for being together was to reflect God in their togetherness as His creation.

The second thing Adam experienced was an emotional connection with Eve. He said, "bone of my bones, and flesh of my flesh." Although his words may not sound like much to us today, they show Adam's emotional response to what he had just witnessed spiritually.

Third, the Bible says Adam "joined" with Eve, his wife, which is understood to be physical, including sexual intercourse. That was the beginning of their physical intimacy, an expression of intimacy that first began spiritually and then emotionally.

We now see God's pattern and order of intimacy that began between Adam and Eve, man and woman, husband and wife.

1. Adam saw Eve spiritually.
2. Then Adam reached out to Eve emotionally.
3. Lastly, the couple became physically intimate.

In that order, man and woman became as one spirit, soul, and body. The precise order of the three components is essential to man and woman becoming companions in every way, as God intended. When spouses feel lonely in their marriage, they can find the root cause by considering the extent or level of their intimacy—spiritually, emotionally, and sexually—and evaluating the priority and order of that threefold connection.

Many couples have confessed their premarital, out-of-bounds relationships, confirming that very few relationships begin spiritually. More commonly, relationships begin emotionally or sexually.

Understanding God's plan for marital relationships prompts couples to ask God to help them reorder and reprioritize their need for spiritual intimacy.

Key Thought:

Your relationship with your spouse should first be **spiritual**, then **emotional**, and then **sexual**.

When and how did your spiritual, emotional, and sexual relationship begin with your spouse? Do you need to make any changes today?

3. SPIRITUAL INTIMACY WITH GOD IS ESSENTIAL

I pray that the Father of glory, the God of our Lord Jesus Christ, would impart to you the riches of the Spirit of wisdom and the Spirit of revelation to know him through your deepening intimacy with him. (Eph. 1:17, TPT)

Many Christians say they want spiritual intimacy with their spouses, but very few seem to be experiencing it.

> *Unless you develop spiritual intimacy with God and each other, any changes in your emotional and sexual relationships will be temporary and less than what God wants for you.*

You may believe being born again creates spiritual intimacy with God, but salvation is only the beginning, like unlocking a door to a room. Walking through an open door isn't the same as exploring every nook and cranny or living in the room. Likewise, many who receive Jesus Christ into their lives consider their salvation as "fire insurance" rather than a *new life* in Christ, made possible by the indwelling of the Holy Spirit. They don't realize that after the door to new life is unlocked, they must explore what's on the inside to experience that new life.

In the following passage, it's interesting that Paul is praying for *believers* rather than unbelievers to have intimate relationships with God.

> I pray that he would unveil within you the unlimited riches of his glory and favor until supernatural strength floods your innermost being with his divine might and explosive power. Then, by constantly using your faith, the life of Christ will be released deep inside you, and the resting place of his love will become the very source and root of your life. Then you will be empowered to discover what every holy one experiences—the great magnitude of the astonishing love of Christ in all its dimensions. How deeply intimate and far-reaching is his love! How enduring and inclusive it is! Endless love beyond measurement that transcends our understanding—this extravagant love pours into you until you are filled to overflowing with the fullness of God! (Eph. 3:16–19, TPT)

Do you see how intimacy with God is so much more than just taking the first step into being born again? Although the first step is essential, it's just the beginning!

Paul encouraged the believers to grasp this amazing truth. He prayed for their intimacy with God to transcend their natural understanding, to the point that they would overflow with the fullness of God!

Recalling that *intimacy* is "into-me-see," God already *sees into you* completely because you are "open and laid bare to him" (Heb. 4:13). The question is whether you're fully seeing into God. Seeing into God has the power to change your life and marriage.

Consider these biblical encounters:

- Moses saw the burning bush.
- Ezekiel saw the wheel.
- Jacob saw the ladder into heaven.
- Isaiah saw God "high and lifted up" (Isa. 6:1).
- The disciples saw Jesus's transfiguration.
- Paul saw the bright light on the road to Damascus.
- John saw God's revelation about the end times.

Each saw God through spiritual eyes, and the experience affected their thinking, feelings, and actions for the rest of their lives.

The same principle applies to us.

> *If you want to experience spiritual intimacy with your spouse, you must start with seeing and hearing God for yourself.*

Just like being born again unlocks a door to spiritual intimacy with God, marriage unlocks a door to spiritual intimacy with your spouse. But this assumes you have been "born again" (saved). This step allows you to experience spiritual intimacy first with God and then with your spouse.

We've seen many situations where a spouse was unhappy with the spiritual intimacy in their marriage, only to eventually discover that their spouse had never actually been born again. It's an essential first step.

🔑 Key Thought:

Your spiritual intimacy with God is the **starting point** for your spiritual intimacy together.

How did your spiritual journey with God begin?

4. SPIRITUAL INTIMACY FUELS YOUR MARRIAGE

If we walk in the light as He Himself is in the Light, we have fellowship with one another, and the blood of Jesus His Son cleanses us from all sin. (1 John 1:7)

The Bible frequently uses a "walking" metaphor to symbolize how we move through our day-to-day activities. Walking in the light of Jesus is an intimate spiritual walk with Him. His presence illuminates our paths, reveals our directions, exposes our thoughts and feelings, and gauges our decisions.

Walking in the light of Christ is a life of complete transparency fueled by His Holy Spirit. God promises if we "walk in the light" with our spouses, we'll experience intimate fellowship, oneness, harmony, communion, and sharing—without guilt, shame, and condemnation because we're also experiencing the cleansing power of Jesus's blood.

That's the picture of intimacy and oneness God designed for marriage, but few people understand the importance and vibrancy of spiritual intimacy with their spouses. They know their relationship with God is spiritual, but they believe, primarily by example, that their relationship is limited to emotional and sexual experiences. And by example and teaching, they reserve spiritual times *alone* rather than together, as a couple, with God. As a result, they experience very little, if any, spiritual intimacy with their spouse. The couple typically doesn't ever reach the vibrant, fulfilling spiritual connection God intended for marriage.

Attempts to become spiritually intimate can feel awkward, as most marriages began with a sexual focus that then moved toward emotional fulfillment. Because infatuation and sex are so much fun at the beginning of the relationship, couples typically delight in this emotional high for about eighteen months. When the excitement fades, the unity begins to deteriorate, and spouses move toward isolation. Isolation is separation resulting from the lack of a spiritual foundation to support and build the relationship.

Spouses then evaluate their marriages principally on how well their emotional and sexual needs are being met: Is my marriage interesting, exciting, and sexually fun?

Relationships consumed by sex and emotional fulfillment have no available space to establish and build spiritual intimacy. This lack creates a spiritual facade among many churchgoing couples, as their emotional and sexual connection can be mistaken in their outward appearance as a strong spiritual intimacy.

We've seen spouses struggle to develop a spiritual relationship because they think attending church lays the foundation and builds spiritual intimacy. But typically, church results in very little spiritual communication between them, except for the occasional joint critique of the pastor's message. Fleeting, if not rare, are moments spent in processing together what God is doing in each other's life spiritually. And prayer, if any, happens perfunctorily before meals with just one spouse (or child) praying aloud rather than heart-engaged communication with God together as a couple and family.

Even "quiet times" ironically suggest and promote an individual pursuit of God rather than the couple's united pursuit of God. Certainly, having a quiet time is an excellent practice, but not meant to be exclusively experienced alone. In fact, God's Word tells us to "pursue righteousness, faith, love, and peace *with those who call on the Lord from a pure heart*" (2 Tim. 2:22, emphasis added). The best person to pursue God with is your spouse, remembering that the marriage relationship of two individuals united them as one in every regard—spiritually, emotionally, and sexually.

We were not designed to be satisfied solely through emotional and sexual intimacy. Although human spiritual connection is a great mystery, we long for spiritual intimacy with our spouses. Marriage unlocks the door for a spiritual relationship between husbands and wives because God designed marriage to be spiritually intimate first.

Constructing spiritual groundwork is essential to enable the relationship to foster and feed the emotional and sexual intimacy and to withstand challenges and changes that occur throughout marriage. To lay a spiritual foundation to build on, we must learn how to engage with each other spiritually. We'll walk you through the foundation laying in the following pages.

Key Thought:

Spiritual intimacy is the **fuel**, emotional intimacy is the **gauge**, and sexual intimacy is the **expression** of both.

How satisfied are you with the spiritual intimacy in your marriage?

---

5. EVALUATE YOUR SPIRITUAL INTIMACY

ACTIVITY: SEVEN AREAS OF SPIRITUAL INTIMACY

After the following scale, review the Seven Areas of Spiritual Intimacy, and rate how well you're doing in each area.

- 9: Completely or extremely
- 8: Strongly (almost always)
- 7: A great deal
- 6: Very much
- 5: A fair amount
- 4: Somewhat (not often)
- 3: Slightly
- 2: Very little
- 1: Not at all

a. Bearing and sharing each other's burdens.

Help carry one another's burdens, and in this way, you will obey the law of Christ. (Gal. 6:2, GNT)

A spiritually intimate couple is better equipped to help each other with their worries, burdens, and weaknesses. Of course, for your spouse to bear your burden, you must share the burden with them. Your spouse cannot help bear the burdens you hold in secret.

Out of the abundance of the heart the mouth speaks." (Matt. 12:34, ESV)

When you share a burden, you may easily let your spouse know how you feel, but you may struggle with being honest about your *spiritual* condition. While sharing emotions is important, identifying and sharing your spiritual condition will move you more quickly to healing.

Living life on the "low road" of humility results in our willingness to share our weaknesses, temptations, and struggles and ask for help in all three areas of our lives: spirit, soul, and body.

Rating: _____

b. Meditating on God's Word and sharing what it's doing inside you.

Just as you have always obeyed, not as in my presence only, but now much more in my absence, work out your own salvation with fear and trembling; for it is God who is at work in you, both to desire and to work for His good pleasure. (Phil. 2:12–13)

The standard and perpetual church answer to spiritual growth and personal relationship with God seems to be, "Read your Bible and pray." Sometimes we tune out this essential *starting point* and fail to engage in these foundational practices with our spouses. We must remember that meditating on God's Word changes how we think, feel, and act. Meditating on God's Word with our spouses is a foundational building block to spiritual intimacy in marriage.

The word of God is alive and powerful. It is sharper than the sharpest two-edged sword, cutting between soul and spirit, between joint and marrow. It exposes our innermost thoughts and desires. (Heb. 4:12, NLT)

The Word of God has the power to change you and your marriage. But you must read and contemplate it as individuals and as a couple.

> To experience spiritual intimacy with your spouse, you need to share how God's Word is affecting your life and how the Holy Spirit is at work inside of you, changing you.

- Beware of gaining knowledge to puff up yourself (1 Cor. 8:1), but rather have the mindset to receive a revelation from God that will change your thinking, feelings, and behaviors. If these three changes don't happen when you and your spouse read God's Word, you've only had a casual interaction with Scripture, even though you may have gained intellectual knowledge.
- Warning: An intellectual approach to God and His Word can result in a self-righteous attitude without you ever realizing or recognizing the supernatural power of God to change your life. When your heart is open to God's Word in meditation, the supernatural power of the Word will define and change the thoughts and intentions of your heart.

What does *meditate* mean? It's like a cow chewing cud. She eats the grass but then brings it back up to chew and chew again.

To receive a revelation from God, we need to do more than just read the Bible. We need to think, consider, ponder, and reflect on what God is saying and how His truths apply to our lives as individuals and couples pursuing spiritual intimacy with them.

Scripture is sometimes better absorbed by meditating on one verse than by reading an entire chapter.

God's Word can reshape your hopes and dreams, and sharing with your spouse what God's Word is doing inside you creates spiritual intimacy with them.

Rating: _____

c. Encouraging your spouse that God has given them the power to overcome sin.

Encourage one another every day, as long as it is still called "today," so that none of you will be hardened by the deceitfulness of sin. (Heb. 3:13)

We know that our old sinful selves were crucified with Christ so that sin might lose its power in our lives. We are no longer slaves to sin. For when we died with Christ we were set free from the power of sin. (Rom. 6:6–7, NLT)

The devil's three goals are deception, discouragement, and despair. One way he hits us with these is by lying. He whispers that we have no choice but to sin. When our old patterns and addictions begin to take over, we tend to believe the lie, which leads us to feel powerless to stop, and we become discouraged, even to the point of despair in our very lives.

Our journey to freedom through Jesus Christ—"the way, the truth, and the life" (John 14:6)—often starts with our spouses' encouraging reminders that we can indeed be free.

Encourage your spouse to persevere and believe what God said is true: Jesus has freed them from the power of sin! Freedom through Christ includes:

- pointing out lies to your spouse that they're believing
- encouraging your spouse to substitute Satan's lies with the truth of God's Word
- speaking that truth to your spouse verbatim
- declaring to your spouse that God has given them the power to overcome any sin and obstacle

No one has more at stake in your spouse's freedom from sin than you. And no one can encourage your spouse more than you because no one loves your spouse more. This type of encouragement in a marriage will help create spiritual intimacy and hope for a better future.

Rating: _____

d. Participating in the healing of your spouse.

> Confess your sins to one another, and pray for one another so that you may be healed. A prayer of a righteous person, when it is brought about, can accomplish much. (James 5:16)

On their wedding day, excited grooms and brides eagerly declare their marriage will change the world and last forever. Of course, many have kept their flaws hidden and promoted their strengths. So those couples enter marriage in a state of wedded bliss, ignorant of what may lie under the surface.

But at some point within their first few years as husband and wife, most will see that their spouses have some level of brokenness, whether caused by dysfunctional upbringings or simply by living in this fallen world.

God wants your marriage to be far more than surface companionship and raising a family. He wants your marriage relationship to be abundant and life-giving, which includes fostering a relationship of healing. He wants to use each spouse to minister healing over the other spouse's brokenness.

You can participate with God in healing your spouse by hearing their confessions and praying for their healing. The wounded spouse must first reveal all brokenness. Then discuss, examine, and pray over each aspect. Few actions will create more spiritual intimacy than being used by God in the healing of your spouse.

Rating: _____

e. Worshipping together.

> Do not get drunk with wine, in which there is debauchery, but be filled with the Spirit, speaking to one another in psalms and hymns and spiritual songs, singing and making melody with your heart to the Lord; always giving thanks for all things in the name of our Lord Jesus Christ to our God and Father; and subject yourselves to one another in the fear of Christ. (Eph. 5:18–21)

Do you worship together? Do you regularly seek and experience God's presence with your spouse? Do you sing together? Do your relationship and family include speaking together in song? If your answer is "Yes, at church," you're missing the point. Worshipping together should happen more often at home than at church.

Singing worship songs together is an intimate activity that many couples don't do. But worshipping together has the power to draw you closer in every amazing way. Try singing together out loud. You may feel awkward at first, but you'll learn to love it.

What about your body posture during worship? For example, raising your hands, kneeling, lying prostrate, clapping, and shouting. Are you comfortable showing humility and praise to God through your body in front of your spouse?

Your physical manifestations of worship should be the outcome of being filled with the Holy Spirit. Physical movement can be an indicator of the vibrancy of your vertical relationship with God and your horizontal relationship with your spouse.

Set aside time to worship together by incorporating singing, praying, posturing your body for worship, and expressing worship to God physically. You'll be amazed how these actions will impact your spiritual intimacy with God and your spouse.

Rating: _____

f. Praying together.

It's surprising how few couples pray together, other than during church activities, mealtimes, weddings, and funerals. Prayer creates spiritual intimacy because listening to your spouse's spiritual conversations with God allows you to see deeper inside them. Prayer is one of the most intimate spiritual activities and can tremendously affect your emotional and sexual intimacy.

When you pray aloud with your spouse, consider these points:

- You're talking to God, not preaching a sermon to each other. Some spouses (mostly wives) feel reprimanded by their spouses during prayer, which creates a reluctance to pray.
- Don't use big, flowery words or your "prayer voice," which can seem pretentious and make your spouse feel like they don't know how to pray. Prayer should be from the mindset and heartset of honesty in conversation with God, your Father.
- There's no formula for praying together.
    - Either spouse can start, and either can end.
    - You can pray more than once.
    - You can pray back and forth in natural, conversational prayer, agreeing with each other's prayers.
    - Intermittent, contemplative silence is okay too.
    - Your prayers can be long or short.
- Don't worry about figuring out the "right way" to pray. Let God lead you, and be attentive to His Spirit.
- If you don't know what or how to pray, ask the Holy Spirit to help you. God wants to help you with your prayers (Rom. 8:26). You may be amazed about what you pray!
- Find a convenient time. If you don't plan, you typically won't pray together.
- If you miss a day, don't allow inner condemnation. Praying together is an opportunity for spiritual intimacy, not an obligation.

- Your children should see you praying together. Seeing Dad and Mom pray creates security in them, teaches them that speaking to God is part of daily life (like speaking to each other), and reveals your relationship and thoughts with God, the Father.

Interestingly, many couples with troubled marriages spend very little, if any, time together in prayer. Often, the first time some couples have prayed out loud in intercession for each other was in a counselor's office. Don't let this happen to you!

Prayer is a first step toward spiritual intimacy. If you haven't yet begun to pray together regularly, we encourage you to start.

Rating: _____

g. Listening for God to speak through your spouse.

Because men frequently believe women are inferior, husbands sometimes don't realize how much power their wives' words have. Whispers from the Holy Spirit can frequently come from your spouse's lips.

Being open to hearing from God through your spouse tells them you trust them, respect their opinion, and believe they're your spiritual equal.

Perhaps you believe your spouse isn't very spiritually rooted, so you wonder how you can take their advice. Your mindset in prayer together is to trust God to reveal Himself through the spouse He's given you. You're honoring your spouse and trusting God to use them in your life and marriage. Even if you think their advice is bad, honoring and trusting God is good.

Rating: _____

6. BARRIERS TO SPIRITUAL INTIMACY

ACTIVITY: SIX BARRIERS TO SPIRITUAL INTIMACY

After the following scale, review the Barriers to Spiritual Intimacy, and use the scale to rate how much each of the six barriers have affected your marriage.

- 9: Completely or extremely
- 8: Strongly (almost always)
- 7: A great deal
- 6: Very much
- 5: A fair amount
- 4: Somewhat (not often)
- 3: Slightly
- 2: Very little
- 1: Not at all

a. Waiting on your spouse to take the first step.

Wives can sometimes be frustrated because their husbands aren't taking responsibility for the spiritual leadership in the home. Believing they should wait on their husbands, they don't take responsibility for their own spiritual growth.

In the same way, husbands can also be overly reliant on their wives. Men can tend to see their wives as responsible for the spiritual activities of the family, such as making sure the kids go to church, praying with them at night, and helping them read and memorize Bible verses.

God wants you to pursue a relationship with Him—without waiting for your spouse to take the first step. When one spouse relies on the other for spiritual growth in their marriage and family, their spiritual intimacy with God and each other suffers. Each spouse must take responsibility for their spiritual growth, and each must take the initiative to grow spiritual intimacy within their marriage and family.

Rating: _____

b. Keeping secret sins hidden.

> There is no creature hidden from His sight, but all things are open and laid bare to the eyes of Him to whom we must answer. (Heb. 4:13)

We spent the first several sessions of this study unpacking your emotional baggage to free yourself from barriers to spiritual intimacy. Coming clean from emotional baggage is an ongoing process because it's easy to start hiding again as the years go by.

Nothing is hidden from God, so nothing should be hidden from your spouse. God wants you to remain HOT with each other forever after. Don't repack your bags!

Rating: _____

c. Thinking you know more than your spouse.

> Knowledge makes one conceited, but love edifies people. If anyone thinks that he knows anything, he has not yet known as he ought to know. (1 Cor. 8:1–2)

A frequent barrier to spiritual intimacy is one spouse acting spiritually superior over the other spouse. The prideful one may ridicule their spouse's thoughts and point out how their spouse doesn't pursue God enough, worship right, sing right, pray right, or serve enough. In other words, one spouse is pointing out how the other can be a better Christian.

Such self-righteous thoughts and feelings mirror the Pharisees. Jesus's harshest words were directed toward them.

Self-righteous spiritual pride will create a significant barrier to spiritual intimacy.

Rating: _____

d. Always conducting spiritual pursuits in private.

> Flee from youthful lusts and pursue righteousness, faith, love, and peace with those who call on the Lord from a pure heart. (2 Tim. 2:22)

Culture in many parts of the world signals that religious thoughts should be kept private. Even laws and policies for business and school make us feel like we can't talk about spiritual matters in those environments. And as we discussed earlier, our daily moments with God are sometimes called "quiet times," reinforcing that spirituality should be private.

While there is an essential benefit to solitude in the pursuit of God, 2 Timothy 2:22 makes clear that there is also benefit in pursuing spiritual matters "with those who call on the Lord from a pure heart."

Look at your calendar and daily routine. Do you have any time with your spouse when you share spiritual thoughts? If not, this is a significant barrier to ever achieving spiritual intimacy.

Rating: _____

e. Apathy toward God.

> My message and my preaching were not in persuasive words of wisdom, but in demonstration of the Spirit and of power, so that your faith would not rest on the wisdom of mankind, but on the power of God. (1 Cor. 2:4–5)

Many people are apathetic toward God or don't believe there is a God because they've never experienced His supernatural work in their lives. Many Christians intellectually study God but seldom experience His real power.

When we move from seeing and hearing God with natural eyes and ears to seeing and hearing Him with spiritual eyes and ears, we're transformed, and feel spiritually alive, filled, and overflowing. His power rids us of apathy and fills us with life. His power changes everything.

If you are apathetic toward God, ask Him for a fresh revelation of His power in your life. Jesus came to open blind eyes and deaf ears. While He certainly did this for some people's physical eyes and ears (as we see in the Bible), much more important to Jesus was opening people's spiritual eyes and ears.

God's fresh revelation of His power is available for all to receive. But we must ask God for His power and, by faith, rely on His Holy Spirit to supply His power in our lives.

Rating: _____

f. Occult involvement.

> "Men and women among you who act as mediums or who consult the spirits of the dead must be put to death by stoning. They are guilty of a capital offense." (Lev. 20:27, NLT)

God made our spirits naturally hungry for spiritual knowledge and life through Him. However, we can easily be drawn astray by lies that make us believe there is spiritual knowledge and life apart from God and His Word. We see examples by so many people drawn to fortune tellers, tarot cards, palm readers, other occult experiences, and religions and spiritual-enlightenment groups that deny Jesus Christ, God, and the living power of His Word. Thoughts, promises, and knowledge contradictory to God's Word are counterfeits rooted in and preoccupied with darkness and death, even though they may appear otherwise. Satan is the great deceiver.

Any practices and pursuits that deny God and His Word can crack open a spiritual door that allows demons to affect how you see and experience life. Instead of leading you to God's light and life, you'll be led into darkness and feelings of death.

Do the activity below, and then provide your rating.

Rating: _____

ACTIVITY:

1. Checkmark every occult practice you have experienced.

	Astral projection (out-of-body experiences)		Satan worship
	Crystal ball		Trances
	Table or body lifting		Voodoo
	Magic eight ball		Drum circle
	Ouija board		Imaginary playmate
	Using spells or curses		Mind control
	Mental control of others		Speaking in a trance
	Automatic writing		Visionary dreams
	Spirit guides		Ghosts
	Fortune-telling		Materialization
	Tarot cards		Clairvoyance
	Palm reading		Mental suggestion
	Tea leaves		Hearing voices in your mind
	Coffee grounds		Mind swapping
	Amulets		Fetishism (objects of worship)
	Charms		Visualization
	Omens		Transcendental meditation
	Astrology/horoscope		Magic rituals
	Hypnosis		Bloody Mary (séance)
	Séances		Occult music (glorifies Satan)
	Black or white magic		Association with people in witchcraft
	Dungeons & Dragons		Use of magic healing
	Fantasy role-playing games		Water witching/dowsing
	Games involving occult power		Occult books or movies
	Blood pacts		Telepathy

SESSION 5: EXPERIENCING SPIRITUAL INTIMACY • 87

Good luck charms	Indian occult rituals
Sexual spirits	Dance with spirits
New age medicine	Sweat lodge purification
Consulted a spiritist	Earth worship
Consulted a medium	Guardian spirits
Consulted a psychic	Spirit travel
Spiritistic healing	Casting magic spells
Witchcraft	Other:

2. As you look at your check-marked items, ask God to show you any lingering impacts on your life.

3. In prayer, renounce each activity and its impact, commanding any demonic influence on your life to leave in Jesus's name.

4. Trust God for a complete release of any remaining bondage.

After the group session, turn to Appendix A and complete your Two-Minute Takeaway.

Session 5: Homework Assignment

When did you decide to stop following your self-designated path and begin following Jesus? To *follow* Jesus means to be *saved* (born again spiritually).

Your *decision* to follow Jesus happened at a specific point in time. In the following journaling space, describe when you made that decision, how your decision occurred, and how your decision changed your life. Discuss your answers with your spouse.

If you can't recall a decision to follow Jesus, you can make that decision right now to receive Jesus into your heart and life by faith, giving Him leadership over your life. The Bible says, "Everyone who calls on the name of the Lord will be saved" (Rom. 10:13), and when "you confess with your mouth Jesus as Lord, and believe in your heart that God raised Him from the dead, you will be saved" (Rom. 10:9).

Understand that the decision of salvation is not a matter of you repeating words. Salvation is:

- recognizing in your heart that you have sinned against God
- agreeing that God is fully justified to judge you for your sins, even to the point of death (Rom. 6:23), but that Jesus, through His death on the cross, paid the penalty for your sins, and all you need to do is receive what Christ did on your behalf (John 1:12)
- changing the direction of your life by following Him, His ways, and His truths, in your thoughts, decisions, actions, reactions, and responses; loving what He loves; and hating what He hates

If you have never called on the name of the Lord and confessed with your mouth, utilize the journaling space to write a prayer of repentance and faith to God, asking Him to save you. Cover the following points in your own words:

- You have sinned and can't do anything to pay for your sins on your own.
- You deserve to be judged by God for the things you have done.
- You are ready to turn your life around and begin following Jesus as your Lord.
- You believe Jesus died for your sins, fully paying the price for your sins, and that God raised Him from the dead on your behalf.
- Ask Jesus to save you and fill you with His Holy Spirit.
- Thank Him for saving you!

Now, pray your prayer out loud with your spouse, and celebrate your new life in Jesus!

1. With your spouse, compare your ratings of items covered in the group session (your level of spiritual intimacy in marriage and barriers to spiritual intimacy).

   Discuss differences in your ratings, and decide what you would like to do to improve.

   Record below any commitments you make to improve your spiritual intimacy with God and your spouse.

   _____
   _____
   _____
   _____

2. Review the occult activities checklist with your spouse. For each activity experienced, share what happened and any impact on your life.

   Pray with your spouse about each occult activity, renouncing each by formally declaring you will no longer participate in the activities and that any hold or impact on your life is now broken in the name of Jesus.

3. With your spouse, review your Two-Minute Takeaway and record action steps.

   Identify at least one thing you want to start doing to improve your spiritual relationship with God and each other. Decide when you will do it and how often.

   > *You are now over halfway through the Savage Marriage Study Guide!*

4. From the first five sessions, review your Two-Minute Takeaways.

   a. Identify the top two to three things you've done or realized that have positively affected your marriage:

      1) _____
      2) _____
      3) _____

   b. Identify the top two to three things you're still working on to positively impact your marriage:

      1) _____
      2) _____
      3) _____

SESSION 6:
CREATING EMOTIONAL INTIMACY

Excerpt from *Savage Marriage*

Priscilla

I had never experienced so many spiritual things happening simultaneously in our life. We were experiencing God's presence in our relationship, in our family, and in the church body where God had placed us.

Our time together in the mornings was real, with God revealing His Word and showing us His heart. We were having an adventure with our heavenly Father each day, and I began to see myself the way He sees me.

Every day was a supernatural experience, and His love toward me was overwhelming. I felt like I'd been dropped into a sea of His love. I was His special daughter, highly favored, standing before Him in His confidence and righteousness. I was not the lowly worm as I had seen—not good enough, smart enough, or desirable enough. I was the daughter of the Eternal King, no longer a prisoner of my shame and secrets. I was totally freed and anointed by Him.

God was using Phil to plant words of life in me, which had not been the norm for us over the past twenty-eight years. His words were refreshing and real and still ring true today. I believe what Phil says about me—"You have power on your head"—because the power is from my heavenly Abba, who gives so freely.

After Phil came clean, my emotional relationship with him blossomed from a molecule of almost nothingness into a beautiful vibrant flower. The change didn't happen overnight or even within weeks. It happened over months of dedicated time through sweat and tears. Change was a painstaking effort to get to know each other in the emotional sense like never before.

When dating, you think you know the person emotionally, but it's just the first layer of emotions. Everything seems great, nothing can go wrong, and you conclude this person makes you feel good. Nothing could be further from the savage reality of what lies ahead in the context of lifelong marriage.

Digging in, leaning into, and pulling out all that encompasses a person and their emotions is not easy in one's natural strength. But in Christ, His grace, compassion, and empathy can take you on a marvelous journey. It was clear that our new emotional intimacy was a result of the spiritual fuel we were now drinking. It felt wonderful.

1. EMOTIONS MAKE US FEEL ALIVE

While spiritual intimacy—with God and each other—is the fuel of marriage, emotional intimacy is the gauge, connecting hearts to create feelings of togetherness, sharing, vulnerability, transparency, mutual respect, and understanding. Emotions bring richness to life. When marriage lacks emotional intimacy, the relationship feels meaningless, numb, and dead.

Self-help books say emotional intimacy and sexual intimacy are the glue of marriage and that we should focus on date nights, recreation, and having more sex. Many people substitute increased recreation and entertainment for true emotional intimacy. But even if you spend day and night consumed with activities, if you don't really know each other, all the activities in the world will eventually become routine.

Activity is not what couples most crave. They long for spiritual and emotional closeness—a real union of their souls. In other words, we want to know our spouses completely and be known completely while being accepted, loved, and respected.

But how do we get there?

The key is putting spiritual intimacy with each other first because the Word of God judges the thoughts and intentions of our hearts. When we share our spirituality with our spouses, we take a giant step toward emotional intimacy.

> The word of God is living and active, and sharper than any two-edged sword, even penetrating as far as the division of soul and spirit, of both joints and marrow, and able to judge the thoughts and intentions of the heart. (Heb. 4:12)

Key Thought:

Emotional intimacy is being completely **known** and confident that you are still **accepted**, **loved**, and **respected**.

How satisfied are you with the emotional intimacy with your spouse?

2. EMOTIONS SHOW WHAT'S INSIDE

> A person's thoughts are like water in a deep well, but someone with insight can draw them out. (Prov. 20:5, GNT)

Our outwardly displayed emotions are evidence of what we're thinking and feeling inside. If you're uncomfortable around other people's emotions, your tendency may be to avoid them (including your spouse) or quickly console them to help get their emotions under control. Instead, ask insightful questions to uncover what's going on inside them. Examples:

- What are you thinking and feeling?
- When was the first time you felt this way?
- How often do you feel this way?
- What happened in your life to make you think and feel this way?
- When you feel this way, what does it make you want to do?
- What do these feelings make you believe about yourself?

Many people have difficulty describing their feelings. A feelings wheel can help you articulate your emotions from a deeper level, below surface descriptions such as *happy*, *mad*, or *sad*. (Many versions of the feelings wheel are available on the internet.)

Lack of emotional intimacy means the relationship *feels* dead. But this doesn't mean the marriage will end in divorce. Many spouses become roommates in perfunctory, legalistic relationships with little or no emotional fulfillment. Some then seek other people to connect with emotionally—including their kids, friends, and lovers—or pursue activities such as hobbies and overworking.

> *Marriages begin with the birth of emotional intimacy and die with the death of emotional intimacy.*

- Emotional intimacy is created when both spouses transparently disclose to each other who they are on the inside while simultaneously extending their acceptance, love, and respect.
- Emotional intimacy mirrors your relationship with your Heavenly Father, who loves you unconditionally and shares all that He is and all that He has.
- Emotional intimacy meets your greatest needs: feeling loved and accepted regardless of who you are, what you disclose, and how you perform.

Conflict will naturally rise and can feel like a threat to your emotional intimacy. However, you get to choose how you will see and utilize conflict. You can allow opposition to steal your emotional intimacy or be your biggest opportunity for emotional growth and deeper intimacy.

Rather than running toward isolation in the middle of a conflict, learn to engage your spouse emotionally through questions. Get your feelings wheel, and describe how you feel. Ask your spouse to describe their feelings and practice accepting, loving, and respecting your spouse's thoughts and feelings.

Consistently using your internal God-given gauge—emotional intimacy—will keep you informed of your marriage's direction. When a potential crisis is on the horizon, you won't be unaware. You'll hear the alarm, call on God to help you reengage in being HOT about your thoughts and feelings, and help you extend acceptance, love, and respect. God is the giver of emotional life, not death. He desires to see you thrive in your marriage.

> ♀ *Key Thought:*
>
> Insightful **questions** can transform an emotional **outburst** into emotional **intimacy**.
>
> How do you respond to an emotional outburst from your spouse?

3. EMPATHY AND COMPASSION ARE THE DOORS TO EMOTIONAL INTIMACY

Rejoice with those who rejoice, and weep with those who weep. (Rom. 12:15)

Empathy and compassion are closely related but have different meanings. Both are doors to emotional intimacy with your spouse.

- Empathy is the ability to understand and relate to another person's feelings.
- Compassion comes from deeper within. Greek meanings for *compassion* include "to be moved in the inward parts"[1] and "visceral compassions"—the compassion God feels toward us,[2] "as if in the internal organs of the body."[3] When you feel true compassion (God's compassion) toward someone, your concern is so deep, on a cellular level, that your emotion impacts your body physically and chemically, moving you to laugh or cry with the individual.

We're drawn to people who exuberantly laugh when we laugh and weep when we weep. We feel emotionally intimate with those who mirror our emotions. We laugh and cry with our closest friends, but the vulnerability associated with crying creates deeper emotional connections.

The opposite occurs when religious and self-righteous attitudes create barriers to compassion. Jesus confronted the Pharisees for their lack of concern for sinners. He told them, "Now go and learn what this means: 'I desire compassion, rather than sacrifice'" (Matthew 9:13). The Pharisees focused on the high road of religion, consumed by a pious desire to appear more significant than others. Jesus told them that they should be more focused on their inward compassion than fulfilling sacrificial laws, the religious system of the Jews. He wants the same for us—to "go and learn" how to focus on our inward feelings for others rather than our outward posturing.

The apostle Paul urged believers to be both empathetic and compassionate:

Be kind to each other, tenderhearted, forgiving one another, just as God through Christ has forgiven you. (Eph. 4:32, NLT)

As those who have been chosen of God, holy and beloved, put on a heart of compassion [visceral compassions], kindness, humility, gentleness, and patience. (Col. 3:12)

---

[1] Bible Hub, s.v. "compassion," accessed March 18, 2022, https://biblehub.com/greek/4697.htm.
[2] Bible Hub, s.v. "visceral compassions," accessed March 18, 2022, https://biblehub.com/greek/3628.htm.
[3] *Merriam-Webster*, s.v. "visceral," accessed March 18, 2022, https://www.merriam-webster.com/dictionary/visceral.

When your spouse shows you what's going on inside them, you should show empathy and compassion for their situation through your words and countenance. Ask God to help you see your spouse as He does.

When you demonstrate God's compassion, you help your spouse bear their burdens, and they feel your care. Showing indifference or distraction when your spouse shares their pain is detrimental to achieving emotional intimacy and a deterrent to your spouse sharing again.

Thank your spouse for sharing, even when what they shared feels hurtful to you. You don't have to be happy with what your spouse shares, but you both should avoid words of contempt and destructive reactions—the enemy's tools. Your contemptuous response erects barriers against your spouse's willingness to share in the future. To nurture and grow emotional intimacy, gratefully receive all disclosures with a blend of honest emotion (even anger, with self-control), grace, acceptance, love, and respect while seeking to show *empathy*, *compassion*, and *thankfulness*.

🔑 Key Thought:

The doorways to emotional intimacy are **empathy** and **compassion**.

Describe a moment when you experienced your spouse's empathy and compassion.

---

4. COMPASSION MINISTERS HEALING

Bear one another's burdens, and thereby fulfill the law of Christ. (Gal. 6:2)

Confess your sins to one another, and pray for one another so that you may be healed. A prayer of a righteous person, when it is brought about, can accomplish much. (James 5:16)

There are at least a dozen Bible references to the compassion Jesus felt before He performed a miracle. He invested not only physically and spiritually in the lives of people who needed His touch but also emotionally.

When your spouse shares a burden, God wants you to follow Christ's example by providing physical comfort and emotional support. Through compassionate listening, talking, and praying, you can minister emotional and physical salve to your spouse as a participant with God in their healing.

Compassion moves us to pray fervently. Prayer without compassion is perfunctory, legalistic, and meaningless, and our spouses can sense the difference.

You might say your spouse isn't very compassionate. But your humble expressions of brokenness and pain can draw out your spouse's compassion. When you want to feel compassion from your spouse, share your honest and open pain and brokenness with a humble spirit or, in circumstances where you have hurt your spouse, a contrite spirit.

Remember: when you recite your needs like you're "reading the newspaper" or with an attitude of entitlement, your spouse will typically not feel moved to compassion.

> ### 🔑 Key Thought:
>
> **Compassionate** prayer allows you to minister **healing** to your spouse.
>
> How would your spouse describe your ability to show compassion?

5. GOD WANTS TO FREE YOUR EMOTIONS

God created each of us in His likeness, with the capacity to feel—because He feels. The first time God described Himself, He used emotional words to paint a picture of His character. We have an emotional God who doesn't withhold His feelings.

> Then the Lord passed by in front of him [Moses] and proclaimed, "The Lord, the Lord God, compassionate and merciful, slow to anger, and abounding in faithfulness and truth." (Ex. 34:6)

In the New Testament, the apostle Paul used several emotional words when describing what it was like to be filled with the Holy Spirit.

> The fruit of the Spirit is love, joy, peace, patience, kindness, goodness, faithfulness, gentleness, self-control; against such things there is no law. (Gal. 5:22–23)

Many of us repressed our emotions from an early age in response to caregivers and culture, believing emotions were a sign of weakness.

People with past trauma sometimes subconsciously shut down their emotions as a coping mechanism. Since they can't selectively turn off feelings, trauma victims may sometimes turn off all their emotions. While buried and numbed feelings can help shield us from feeling life's lows, we're also unable to feel life's highs. Sadly, we're the epitome of the walking dead.

Emotions allow us to experience the richness of life and connectedness with God and our spouses. When we don't feel the full range of emotions with God and our spouses, we're more likely to turn to other sources to feel alive. These pacifiers can be drugs, alcohol, sex, hobbies, work, shopping, and relationships with other people—temporarily satisfying our needs. When we turn to pacifiers for emotional fulfillment, our spouses sense our disinterest in connecting with them, and we create greater emotional distance.

In this dangerous place of emotional lack, both spouses become more susceptible to relationships with other people who show an interest in them. Emotional shutoff and its tentacles of pacifiers lead to another crazy cycle!

But God can heal and renew us back to life!

[Jesus] came to Nazareth, where He had been brought up; and as was His custom, He entered the synagogue on the Sabbath, and stood up to read. And the scroll of Isaiah the prophet was handed to Him. And He unrolled the scroll and found the place where it was written: "The Spirit of the Lord is upon Me, because He anointed Me to bring good news to the poor. He has sent Me to proclaim release to captives, and recovery of sight to the blind, to set free those who are oppressed, to proclaim the favorable year of the Lord." And He rolled up the scroll, gave it back to the attendant, and sat down; and the eyes of all the people *in the synagogue were intently directed at Him.* Now He began to say to them, "Today this Scripture has been fulfilled in your hearing." (Luke 4:16–21)

Jesus declared four things He came to do:

1. Bring good news to the poor
2. Proclaim release to the captives
3. Provide recovery of sight to the blind
4. Free the oppressed

Notice the fourth is to free the oppressed—the downtrodden, bruised, or crushed. These words describe emotions. Jesus came to do something special in the emotions of believers: "set free." If you or your spouse seem almost incapable of embracing your feelings, there's good news. Jesus can supernaturally free your emotions to enjoy the richness of your life as He intended for your relationship with Him and your spouse. But to be set free, you will need to embrace humility, like a little child.

"Truly I say to you, unless you change and become like children, you will not enter the kingdom of heaven." (Matt. 18:3)

Little children approach people emotionally rather than intellectually. They don't worry about what people think, they don't overthink what they're going to say, they're honest and open, and it's easy to see what's going on inside them. Their lives picture how God wants us to relate to Him and each other.

> *Your emotional connection with your spouse directly indicates your emotional connection with God.*

If you struggle with expressing yourself emotionally to your spouse, you probably find it hard to express your feelings to God. Your emotions with God and your spouse are interconnected. God wants you to have a horizontal relationship with your spouse that mirrors your vertical relationship with Him. Becoming emotionally free will strengthen your ability to relate to your spouse and God and invigorate your relationships with both.

Few people realize that the emotional freedom Jesus provided us is just as important as our spiritual freedom. Without His gift of emotional freedom, the wounded may dwell in numbness and lifeless marriages, void of the abundant emotions that reflect God's character, including compassion and empathy.

If you feel numb and disconnected from God or your spouse, ask the Holy Spirit to show you why and to change you. Jesus came to set free the emotionally oppressed, and His freedom is for you!

> **♀ Key Thought:**
>
> Jesus can supernaturally **free** and **empower** you to connect **emotionally** with Him and your spouse.
>
> Describe your struggles to express yourself emotionally to God and your spouse.

6. YOU NEED A NEW VOCABULARY

Death and life are in the power of the tongue, and those who love it will eat its fruit. (Prov. 18:21)

Just as God connects with us through words, husbands and wives also connect through words. God speaks life to us through His Word and from His Spirit in us, and we need to speak *life* into our spouses through our humble words of genuine compassion, empathy, and other beautiful words of love.

Some of us need a new God-given vocabulary to connect with our spouses' emotions.

King David and King Solomon wrote beautiful words expressing their passions and convictions in Psalms, Proverbs, and Song of Solomon. We can ask God for a new vocabulary, a new way of expressing ourselves and asking questions of our spouses that result in marvelous words about the promises we've made to them, our belief in them, and our confidence in our future together. We can ask God to give us words of life: sincere encouragement, praise, affirmation, compliments, admiration, and insight.

Listen carefully to your spouse's words. Listening means putting down your phone, looking your spouse in the eye, telling them you're paying attention, and hearing them. Give verbal and physical feedback that indicates you heard them completely and accurately and are invested in what they're saying.

Bidding and Catching

Dr. John Gottman has written quite a lot about the concept of bidding and catching. When a spouse says something to get the other's attention, that's a *bid*. If the other spouse responds, it's a *catch*—or *turning toward*, as Gottman says.

> Happy couples turn towards their partners approximately 20 times more than couples in distress during everyday, non-conflict discussions. Newlyweds who were still married six years after their wedding had turned towards each other 86% of the time while in the lab. Those who were divorced six years later, however, had only turned towards each other 33% of the time.[4]

In a typical day, spouses can make over one hundred bids, indicating that bids are integral to our marriages. Whether a bid is caught indicates a couple's level of emotional intimacy. Here are some example bids:

---

[4] Ellie Listsa, "An Introduction to Emotional Bids and Trust," The Gottman Institute, https://www.gottman.com/blog/an-introduction-to-emotional-bids-and-trust/.

- Ouch, that really hurt!
- This is so frustrating!
- You know, I really don't feel like cooking dinner tonight.
- I've got so much laundry to do.
- I'd love to watch a good movie.
- My shoulders are so sore!
- I wish I didn't have to help the kids with their homework tonight.

You must be conscious of bids when you're around your spouse. When you hear a bid, put down whatever you're doing and catch the bid by responding with attentive ears, eyes, verbal responses, and caring actions. If you don't, your spouse will feel unimportant and may speak signals of marital distress like, "You never listen to me. You don't care what I think." Such responses are the alarm sounding (discussed in #2 of this session).

When you hear the alarm, what you're frequently hearing are unspoken bids—pleas for emotional connection. When you hear your spouse's negative words and sounds of exasperation, frustration, anger, sadness, or anxiety, you must follow up with questions that draw out the depth and heart of their thoughts and feelings.

> *Ignored bids create distance. Catches create connections.*

You must also avoid all words of death. These include cursing and words of disgust and contempt.

- Disgust is a strong feeling of disapproval or revulsion.
- Contempt is a mixture of disgust and anger.
- Contempt expresses that you feel the other person, their thoughts, and their feelings are worthless, beneath your consideration, or deserving of scorn. Lies from the enemy!

Words of disgust and contempt are impossible to unhear. They resonate and burrow deep in our souls, building barriers that create destructive emotional distance. It's essential to draw the line at cursing and other words of disgust and contempt and vow *never to* use such words.

You may have already unleashed or received emotional death words and experienced that pain. *God can heal and restore. He is the giver of new life!*

If you have spoken words of death, ask God to help you see the pain your words caused. A humble and contrite apology to your spouse is necessary for their healing and yours.

🔑 Key Thought:

Ask God for a new **vocabulary** to express words that create emotional **intimacy** and **connection** with not only your spouse but your entire family.

How are the words that you speak to your spouse influencing your emotional relationship?

7. KILLERS OF EMOTIONAL INTIMACY

Every word said is an opportunity to build up or tear down our emotional connection. In the same way, our actions can also cultivate or kill emotional intimacy. Consider the following killers, and mark those you're guilty of inflicting. You will use these in your homework.

Isolation	Not talking	Criticism
Cursing	Harsh, abrupt communication style	Condescension
Physical abuse	Demanding to be served	Not expressing appreciation
Not listening	Self-righteousness	Quick to anger
Belittling	Making your spouse the butt of your jokes	No physical touching
Manipulation by withholding sex	Giving attention to others at the expense of your spouse	Ignoring your spouse's advice
Too busy	Disregarding commitments to spend time together	Use of digital devices to escape

After the group session, turn to Appendix A and complete your Two-Minute Takeaway.

Session 6: Homework Assignment

1. What examples of good and bad emotional expressions did you see in your family of origin? How have those affected the ways you express your emotions?

   _____
   _____
   _____

2. What would you want to change in the way your children see emotions expressed by you, by your spouse, and within your family? _____

3. Ask God for some new, beautiful words of emotion to thank your spouse for two compassionate things they've done that positively impacted you. Write those below, and then read them out loud to your spouse using words of gratitude.

   1) _____

   2) _____

4. Review the list of Killers of Emotional Intimacy. For those you're responsible for, own them, and write below an apology for each. Then read them out loud to your spouse.

   _____
   _____
   _____
   _____

5. Using a feelings wheel that you can easily find via an internet search, look together at the outmost circle of feelings. Take turns choosing a feeling at random and expressing the following two statements to your spouse about that feeling. Do at least two rounds each of this exercise. With this as a daily exercise, you'll learn how to best express your feelings and become natural at being in touch with your emotions.

   a. I feel _____ when I _____
      _____. [Describe the situation that makes you feel this way.]

   b. The first time I felt _____ was when I
      _____
      _____.
      [Describe what happened, looking back as far as you can to identify the first time you felt this way.]

6. Share your Two-Minute Takeaway from Session 6, and record reactions and agreed-upon action steps.

Notes

SESSION 7: CHERISHING YOUR SPOUSE

Excerpt from *Savage Marriage*

Phil

Most of my words to Priscilla throughout our previous years of marriage had not been special, God-given words but had principally been words about family logistics, such as who needed to be where and what needed to be done. I had neglected to share beautiful words from God that would assure Priscilla that I cherished her.

One morning I was thinking about 1 Corinthians 11:10. "The woman should have a symbol of authority on her head, because of the angels." This passage had seemed antiquated to me, but I knew there was present purpose and relevance behind all Scripture.

Looking at the Greek word for *authority*, I found it most often translated as *power*. So, I began telling Priscilla she had power on her head.

Affirming Priscilla with God's truth had a tremendous impact on her. After she said or did something profound, I would often place my hand on her head and exclaim, "You have power on your head!"

She began receiving this truth and then believed she did indeed have power on her head. The influence of God's Word through my actions further built her up spiritually, connected us emotionally, and helped her feel cherished.

We've found that our emotional intimacy as husband and wife is impacted not only by what we say to one another but also by the actions we take that make us feel either loved or neglected. In other words, we shouldn't only *say* we love one another but should show actions that demonstrate our love.

Gary Thomas's book *Cherish: The One Word That Changes Everything for Your Marriage* "shows that although there are a countless number of marriages consisting of two people just going through the motions, there are real ways this pattern can be reversed: when husbands and wives learn to cherish one another in their everyday actions and words."[1]

Some of the concepts in this session have been adapted from and inspired by this excellent book, and we recommend it for additional study.

---

1 Gary Thomas, *Cherish: The One Word That Changes Everything for Your Marriage* (Zondervan, 2017), https://garythomas.com/books/cherish/.

1. CHERISHING REQUIRES ACTION

Many wedding vows include the promise to "love and cherish, till death do us part." This commitment is memorable, but the promise to cherish can fade and become forgotten.

Cherish is no longer a commonly used word. Yet it's an essential term to the marriage relationship. *Cherish* means tenderly caring for someone or something. Picture a nursing mom or a bird caring for her young. Tenderness, softness, and deep emotional connection (compassion) create care and concern in the mom, which moves her to caring actions, cherishing her baby.

While *love* is associated more with feelings, *cherish* is related to actions that show love. 1 Corinthians 13:4 says, "Love is patient, love is kind," which means love is not simply a feeling but actions of compassion.

> For God so loved [feeling] the world, that He gave [action] His only Son, so that everyone who believes in Him will not perish, but have eternal life. (John 3:16)

Cherishing embodies compassionate actions that actively extend love and grace as Jesus showed in actions throughout His time on Earth—and as God showed by His action of giving His one and only son, Jesus, to die for us on the cross as payment for our sins.

When we consider these profound acts of cherishing us, we can never doubt His love. His actions proved His ongoing and unfailing love for us.

In the same way, your spouse wants to see cherishing actions that prove your love. When your spouse sees your compassionate actions of cherishing, they will know and feel your love. Your spouse's feelings of love will change how they respond and initiate acts toward you, further creating and nurturing emotional intimacy. Over time, cherishing actions become like heartbeats, a perpetual cycle of cellular-level life in and between you and your spouse as "one."

As we discussed under Myth 3 (women are inferior to men), when a wife says she doesn't feel loved, her husband may respond by saying he provides a home, a car, food, and clothing and works day and night to provide for her and the family. By such responses, he's trying to convince his wife that those actions show he loves her and that she's crazy to think otherwise. But his wife's focus is on her word *feel*. The actions her husband rattled off don't make her *feel cherished* because those actions were impersonal, devoid of compassion—tender concern and care—that would make her *feel* loved.

In addition, sometimes spouses will attempt to cherish by using actions that make *themselves* feel cherished rather than their spouses. For example, a husband may feel cherished when his wife runs an errand for him (especially if his primary love language is acts of service). However, running an errand for her may not make her feel cherished.

Many spouses aren't cherishing each other because they don't yet know what actions make their spouses feel cherished.

- Spend time with your spouse, exploring what makes them feel loved, from most to least.
- Ask whether your current actions show tender care and concern.
- Consider whether your actions evoke a positive emotional response.

You must learn what specific actions make *your spouse* feel cherished and understand that those actions may differ from those that make you feel cherished.

> **🔑 Key Thought:**
>
> When you **cherish** your spouse, your actions make them feel **loved**.
>
> What would your spouse say you need to do more of to make them feel loved?

An excellent discovery tool is for both spouses to take the Love Language quiz at https://www.5lovelanguages.com/quizzes/love-language.

Learning and practicing your spouse's love languages in the order of their innate priorities is an essential means to actively loving and cherishing.

New behaviors may require that we go out of our way to notice our spouses, appreciate them, honor them, and hold them dear—cherish. Holding your spouse dear is to mentally reserve your focus exclusively for them, not allowing your eyes and mind to wander to other things (or people) that can replace your love for your spouse.

With the thought of going out of our way, frame your side-by-side list of five love languages, ordered by highest to lowest rated, and place the frame in your shared bathroom or the kitchen. Also, carry a printed copy of your spouse's top three love languages in a visible compartment of your wallet—an item we each use regularly and when we're out without our spouses. This visual reminder will prompt you into action even when you're apart.

2. CHERISHING IS UNCONDITIONAL

I am giving you a new commandment, that you love one another; just as I have loved you, that you also love one another. By this all people will know that you are My disciples: if you have love for one another. (John 13:34–35)

Some spouses place conditions on cherishing, such as, "I'll act like I love you when you change the way you're acting."

Because none of us can consistently act the right way, though we may try, our marriages can become critically devoid of grace—to the point we feel locked in a prison that demands high performance to *earn* our spouse's love. That scenario is the opposite of "set free" and "abundant life" in Christ. Such actions do not create a place of rest or peace but rather hopeless confinement.

We are not under the bondage of performance to earn God's love, and therefore, we must release our desire to control the performance of our spouses by withholding our love. We must cherish our spouses as Jesus cherishes us: unconditionally.

> 🔑 *Key Thought:*
>
> God wants us to cherish our spouses the way He cherishes us: without **performance**.
>
> Does your spouse believe they need to perform to earn your love? Ask them and describe below.

3. CHERISHING REQUIRES A NEW PATTERN

Do not be conformed to this world, but be transformed by the renewing of your mind. (Rom. 12:2)

Patterns of relating to our spouses are primarily rote and based on our past thoughts and actions. We must relearn seeing our spouses as valuable, treasured, and infinitely loved so nothing else can fill our thoughts and souls more than our spousal relationship and our relationship with Christ.

Changing old patterns of behavior requires vigilance, intention, and practice. But when cherishing arrives in your marriage, you both will feel like the most blessed person alive.

> 🔑 *Key Thought:*
>
> Old behavior patterns may need to **change** to make your spouse feel **cherished**.
>
> What behavior patterns does your spouse need to change?

4. CHERISHING TRANSFORMS YOUR SPOUSE

God didn't send Jesus to die on the cross for us because we deserved His death—we deserved our own death, yet He took our place as full payment for humanity's sin. His death demonstrated His love for us even though we are sinners. God's actions are incarnate cherishing. Through His grace and our obedience to renew our minds, we become transformed to cherish our spouses as Christ cherishes us.

Demonstrating grace to your spouse is part of active cherishing that has the power to help transform them. But some may say, "You don't know what my spouse has done. They don't deserve grace!" Neither did you or any of us, yet God gave us grace anyway. By providing unmerited favor, God opened a path for our transformation. His grace empowered us and made way for us to be more and more like Him. You can extend the same transformative grace to your spouse by offering grace in unconditional love. Complimenting your spouse, for example, does more to change them than criticism. When you praise and admire your spouse, you increase and solidify positive, life-giving, life-changing, marriage-changing behaviors. These actions collaborate with God in the healing of your spouse's wounds.

If you feel like your spouse's shortcomings are always before you, look for one good thing each day that they've said or done, and then express your sincere appreciation and admiration. You'll be amazed how this simple act of cherishing can transform your spouse.

God didn't cherish Israel because they were loveable. He cherished Israel, and they were transformed to be loveable. He wants us to follow this example in our marriage relationships. When we cherish our spouses, they can become transformed by our love.

Key Thought:

Cherishing transforms your spouse from who they **are** into who they **can be**.

Have you seen how cherishing your spouse can change them? Describe.

5. CHERISHING PROTECTS YOUR MARRIAGE

> *Betrayal can be a red flag that calls attention to deficiencies in a relationship that led at least one partner to feel lonely and devalued. (What Makes Love Last?* by John Gottman, Ph.D., and Nan Silver)

Not feeling cherished should never be a pass card to pursue a relationship with the opposite sex. However, not feeling cherished explains why many affairs start. Cherishing your spouse helps to protect your marriage.

Betrayal starts in the mind and emotions within the marriage relationship long before it is consummated. For example, one spouse reneges on their promise to have children or makes their job or hobby more important than spending time with their spouse. Unmet expectations can cause thoughts and feelings of betrayal that crack open the door for an extramarital relationship to start. Feelings and thoughts of betrayal within the marriage create feelings similar to betrayal outside the marriage.

Many affairs begin emotionally due to a spouse feeling lonely or devalued (feelings of betrayal), and *then* the spouse meets someone who makes them feel alive. Infidelity may start with a conversation. With continued interest, the connection may take gradual steps that become something more, such as repeated conversations that grow more intimate. Such conversations may include sharing details about spouses.

The intimate sharing leads to lingering looks, physical touches such as a hug or peck on the cheek, meeting for lunch, and further progressing to a physical relationship. Throughout this dance of betrayal, there's an internal comparison of the new relationship to the spousal relationship. This comparison eventually leads the betrayer to conclude that the new relationship is more attractive and exciting than their spouse. The betrayer justifies their adultery by thinking the affair is due to their spouse not showing love to them or otherwise meeting their needs.

When you ignore, criticize, and treat your spouse with contempt, they become vulnerable to someone else making them feel alive.

Cherishing your spouse can help protect your marriage from outside relationships. Cherishing is not foolproof by human nature but follows God's example for us. We love Him because we know and experience His love for us. Loving and cherishing are the patterns set by God for the marriage relationship. "We love, because He first loved us" (1 John 4:19).

When we know, experience, and feel our spouse's love, this cherishing draws us toward them in a way that helps to seal the protection of our marriage, making it difficult for others to get in.

Key Thought:

When one spouse feels **lonely** or **devalued**, it can make them **vulnerable** to anyone who makes them feel **alive**.

Has your marriage been touched by infidelity? What were the circumstances? Has the betrayal been forgiven and healed?

ACTIVITY: CHERISHING MY SPOUSE

Part 1—Rating:

Using the scale below, review the following Cherishing My Spouse exercise, and rate each action based on how well you're cherishing your spouse. (You'll complete Part 2, Ranking, after completing all your ratings.)

- 9: Completely or extremely
- 8: Strongly (almost always)
- 7: A great deal
- 6: Very much
- 5: A fair amount
- 4: Somewhat (not often)
- 3: Slightly
- 2: Very little
- 1: Not at all

a. By the way you speak

Death and life are in the power of the tongue, and those who love it will eat its fruit. (Prov. 18:21)

Every conversation can move you closer to or further from emotional intimacy with your spouse. A conversation full of words of life will create life in your spouse. Conversely, words of death will create death in your spouse. Therefore, the words you speak to your spouse are very important to them feeling cherished, even if "words of affirmation" are at the bottom of their love language list. As the proverb above states, we're impacted positively or negatively by words.

Words of life include sincere encouragement, praise, affirmation, compliments, admiration, and insight. And the tone of your words is a big deal. Often it's not what you say but how you say it.

Be specific—not general—with your praise. When you say your spouse looks good, say why or what you admire. Also, praising your spouse in front of others can be very encouraging.

When you criticize your spouse for things they may be unable to change, you place them in a hopeless situation. So avoid all words directed toward your spouse's past and limitations, such as their body type, personality, and any mental, emotional, and physical restrictions. Never use demeaning words to or about your spouse.

Ask yourself: When I see my spouse, am I scanning them to figure out something good to say or something to criticize? If you don't know, ask your spouse. They can read your body language and will most certainly know what direction your scanning is taking you. Remain on the low road of humility that produces cherishing, compassion, grace, and love.

(Part 1) Rating: _____ (Part 2) Rank: _____

b. By the way you listen

"If anyone has ears to hear, let him hear." (Mark 4:23)

Jesus used this phrase many times, indicating He wanted people to listen to His voice and follow Him. It's interesting that one of God's first commands to the children of Israel was to listen to Him (Ex. 15:26). God gave this command because listening would be the only way Israel could get to know Him.

The same is true in marriage. Listening to your spouse will let you know them better and make them feel respected and important because listening shows that you value what they have to say.

When you're distracted, your spouse feels ignored, and the enemy whispers in their ear, "They're not interested in you. They don't really love or prefer you."

When your spouse is sharing, demonstrate active listening by responding with questions rather than statements.

- Statements reflect a decision, determination, judgment, or accusation you made in your thoughts before responding.
- Questions reflect interest, concern, and a desire to know more, making your spouse feel cherished.

(Part 1) Rating: _____ (Part 2) Rank: _____

c. By the way you <u>serve</u>

>Whoever desires to be first among you shall be your slave; just as the Son of Man did not come to be served, but to serve, and to give His life as a ransom for many. (Matt. 20:27–28)

>Husbands, love your wives, just as Christ also loved the church and gave Himself up for her, so that He might sanctify her, having cleansed her by the washing of water with the word, that He might present to Himself the church in all her glory, having no spot or wrinkle or any such thing; but that she would be holy and blameless. So husbands also ought to love their own wives as their own bodies. He who loves his own wife loves himself; for no one ever hated his own flesh, but nourishes and cherishes it, just as Christ also does the church, because we are parts of His body. (Eph. 5:25–30)

Even Jesus made it clear that He came not to be served but to serve others—the pattern God set for husbands. Husbands should lay down their lives for their wives.

When Jesus gave up His life for us, He made way for us to become transformed. Likewise, when a husband gives up his life for his wife, he makes way for her transformation.

Serving each other in our homes is something everyone should do. Who would your kids say is doing most of the work in your home? Who would you say? Accepting more service from your spouse than you're providing can indicate your pride—your desire to be served. Your pride will build resentment in your spouse and lead to emotional distance.

Ask God to help you cherish your spouse through serving. Ask your spouse where they need help. Surprise them by taking on some things they've been doing. Make selfless serving part of cherishing your spouse.

(Part 1) Rating: _____ (Part 2) Rank: _____

d. By the way you <u>love</u> and <u>respect</u>

>Each husband is to love his own wife the same as himself, and the wife must see to it that she respects her husband. (Eph. 5:33)

While men and women both need love *and* respect, men generally value respect more (because women are good at showing love). Women typically want to feel loved (because men naturally embrace respect by their willingness to die for their family).

God commanded men to love even when love seems undeserved, and He commanded women to respect even when respect seems undeserved. Marriages get stuck when love and respect are withheld—men wanting respect before they show love, and women demanding love before they show respect. The only way to break this cycle is for one spouse to demonstrate humility: die to their desires in favor of showing love or respect to their spouse, without thought of what their spouse deserves. Deserving is *never* part of the equation.

(Part 1) Rating: _____ (Part 2) Rank: _____

e. By the way you <u>touch</u>

Touching can create wonderful physical sensations of love and affection. While most men's minds go quickly toward sexual touching, a woman's mind will frequently go to nonsexual touching. Most men need to focus more on nonsexual touching to create feelings of emotional intimacy in their spouses.

Men also love nonsexual touching and genuinely appreciate their wives initiating touch. However, some wives refrain from touching when experiences with their spouses have taught them that their husbands will interpret every touch as a desire or invitation for sex.

Notice that a lingering touch can mean more than a routine, brief touch. The next time you greet your spouse, give a lingering hug or kiss rather than a quick peck (if that's your routine).

- Let your spouse know you're not rushing.
- Make the touch nonsexual.
- Enjoy the moment.
- Let your kids see your affection for each other.
- Don't be afraid to show some affection in public. Appropriate PDA is okay!

Sexual touching is also important but needs to flow out of spiritual and emotional intimacy rather than a means to sexual touching. (The next session will cover sexual touching.)

(Part 1) Rating: _____ **(Part 2) Rank:** _____

f. By the <u>time</u> you share

There is no substitute for time spent with your spouse, one on one, without distractions. Giving time to your spouse is a gift no one else can give as you can. Time with your spouse shows them you prefer to be with them rather than anything else. Time together is the ultimate compliment.

Our addictions steal the time and energy we could invest in relationships with our spouse and family. Addictions wreck many marriages.

We must also avoid being consumed by hobbies done alone or with people other than our spouses. This is not to say you shouldn't have individual or group hobbies but rather a caution to carefully evaluate the time impact of your hobbies on your marriage.

Spending quality time each day with your spouse is better for your relationship than a "date night." If you spend an hour with your spouse each day, you'll find that "date night" no longer seems to be the solution to your problems. Dates can be the extra topping, especially for stay-at-home mothers. If your work schedules don't allow for even an hour together, it's crucial to set aside uninterrupted time together each week. Your marriage needs consistent investments of time to flourish, ideally every day.

In scheduling time to be together (yes, get out your calendars, and schedule time), cut out every distraction, including phones, video games, TV, and social media. Some studies have shown that these activities in excess are linked to depression. You'll find that quality time with your spouse will breathe more life into you than all the video games you can play.

(Part 1) Rating: _____ **(Part 2) Rank:** _____

g. By the <u>gifts</u> you give

The most meaningful gifts you can give your spouse are those that reflect your knowledge of them, their likes and dislikes, their desires, and your sacrifice to know your spouse and cherish them with gifts that are meaningful to them. What you like is not typically what your spouse likes.

In many cases, giving something you've thoughtfully made can generate more emotional connection than something you've bought. Making a hurried trip to the drugstore to buy a last-minute gift may harm your relationship more than help. Such gifts tell your spouse that your thoughts of them were last-minute rather than a priority.

Your gift-giving should be generous, which doesn't mean expensive. Generous gifting includes:

- the way you present the gift
- the words you use
- the time you took to make or shop for the gift
- the way the gift reflects your knowledge and honor of your spouse

Special gifts of service also count—for example, arranging a party that will honor your spouse. Investments of your time and heart are far more valuable than financial investments in gifts. Each of the examples above show sacrifice and the cherishing of your spouse.

(Part 1) Rating: _____ **(Part 2) Rank:** _____

Part 2—Ranking:

Go back through this activity's topics, and reflect on how you can cherish your spouse. Then rank each numerically (1–7) based on how important each is toward your spouse feeling cherished. The most important rank is 1, the second-most important is 2, etc. You will use the ranking in the homework.

After the group session, turn to Appendix A and complete your Two-Minute Takeaway.

Session 7: Homework Assignment

1. Individually complete the following template. For the first two columns, transfer your scores from your reading work. These should reflect how much you believe *your spouse feels cherished* by you. Then complete columns three and four based on how much *you feel cherished*.

Ways we feel cherished	**RATE** how much **your spouse** feels cherished by you	**RANK** how important this is to your **spouse**	**RATE** how much **you** feel cherished by your spouse	**RANK** how important this is to **you**
Words				
Listening				
Serving				
Love and Respect				
Touching				
Time				
Gifts				

2. Think of three specific things you can do to help your spouse feel loved and cherished. Write them below. When complete, read them out loud to your spouse. Ask for feedback, and edit below as appropriate. Pray together and ask God to help you make the necessary changes to better cherish your spouse.

   a. _____

   b. _____

   c. _____

3. Share your Two-Minute Takeaway, and record reactions and your agreed-upon action steps in Appendix A.

Notes

SESSION 8:
BECOMING A GIVER, NOT A TAKER

Excerpt from *Savage Marriage*

Phil

I'd had warped sexual expectations going into marriage, which was no surprise. I had thought Priscilla should make me the center of her universe like my imaginary lovers had. When Priscilla had failed to act as I'd imagined, I'd demanded and pouted, leaving her emotionally naked and feeling used.

Although I had sensed Priscilla felt unfulfilled in our marriage, I'd chalked that up to her living a sheltered life. I had been so arrogant and self-centered that I had failed to see I was causing her to retreat from me and our marriage. All those years, I should have seen our sexuality as King Solomon had described his experiences—like preparing and living in a garden (Song of Sol. 5:1).

I had not seen our sex life like a garden that needed preparation—tilling, planting, and care. I had seen our sexual relationship more like a convenience store, available whenever I had run out of what I needed. Though I had settled for convenience, what I'd really wanted (and hadn't realized in those years) was a spiritual and emotional connection with my wife.

Entering our new door of sexuality with my wife was like preparing a garden at the back of our property—disregarded for too long and full of weeds. Our relationship had needed a lot of time, help, and preparation before we could expect to receive anything.

We began the process by looking to the Master Gardener for direction, with faith that if we sowed seeds according to His plan, our garden would indeed produce an excellent, fully satisfying crop of lovely feelings, thoughts, and memories. And that was just what we gleaned.

The weed pulling had included discarding old images that had danced through our heads, and the planting created radiant new memories that called out to us even when we weren't together, reminding us of what was in store when we reconnected. Our new memories were rich and filling, showing us that God's way is far more excellent. After all, He's the Artist, Designer, and Creator of the magnificent gift of sexual intimacy.

> Like Adam and Eve, Priscilla and I then knew the beauty of God's garden. We rejoiced in His presence during our romantic encounters, feeling set free to enjoy all He had planned for us. We gathered our myrrh and balsam, ate our honeycomb and honey, drank our wine and milk, and followed God's encouragement from Song of Solomon 5:1—"Eat, friends; Drink and drink deeply, lovers."

This session explores how sexual intimacy with your spouse should incorporate and reflect the spiritual intimacy you experience with God. Our goal is to help you transform your past pain and shame into something beautiful and sacred shared between you and your spouse.

Sexual intimacy is a very sensitive topic for many couples. Please press into this session. Don't let the pain and shame of your past rob you from experiencing all that God wants to do in your garden of sexual intimacy.

1. SEXUAL INTIMACY FLOWS FROM SPIRITUAL AND EMOTIONAL INTIMACY

Along our savage marriage journey, God showed us His order to intimacy that incorporated our spiritual, emotional, and physical beings.

Remember how Adam began his relationship with Eve?

He first saw a spiritual connection with her as he realized God had created her from him. He then connected to her emotionally through his words ("bone of my bones, and flesh of my flesh"). Later, he consummated his relationship with her sexually. Their relationship followed God's sequence for marriage: spiritual, then emotional, and, lastly, sexual. Due to this order, Adam and Eve's sexual union was the most intimate expression of their spiritual and emotional relationship.

> For this reason a man shall leave his father and his mother, and be joined to his wife; and they shall become one flesh. (Gen. 2:24)

What is the *reason* a man should leave his parents and be joined to his wife? To have kids? To enjoy sex? To make him complete?

No.

In God's view, a man should be joined to his wife because he sees himself as spiritually and emotionally connected to her. Sadly, most marriages don't reflect God's order for developing marriage relationships. But with the Holy Spirit's help, marriages are transformed, reflecting His designed order of intimacy.

God designed marriage to express spouses' intimate spiritual, emotional, and physical knowledge of each other. Even the Hebrew word translated as *sexual intercourse* means "to know."[1]

When you follow God's order of intimacy, you feel wonderful physically, emotionally, and spiritually. Tri-fold intimacy is the one area where spouses realize and experience the full meaning of becoming one flesh.

Of course, the world does not see God's divine order for establishing and building a relationship between spouses. The world's solution to sexual issues is physical technique improvements and increased frequency. Magazines and books are full of advice about how sex can be better through performance changes. But physical changes in sex will produce only physical responses.

---

[1] Bible Hub, s.v. "yada," accessed March 21, 2022, https://biblehub.com/hebrew/3045.htm.

Some couples change their sex lives by adding pornography, sex toys, and even other people in futile attempts to find ultimate satisfaction. But such activities produce only momentary sexual excitement that cannot sustain a constant, new sexual high. Boredom and loss of passion are the eventual and inevitable results. And for Christians, shame and guilt may afterward plague the relationship.

> *Following God's path to sexual intimacy promises true fulfillment without shame or guilt.*

True satisfaction and fulfillment in your sex life, and the answer to your sexual problems, require you and your spouse to be spiritually and emotionally close first in the same way you become spiritually and emotionally "one" with Christ. Sex between husband and wife is the intimate expression of the spiritual and emotional intimacy that can thrive between God and humans. In sexual expression, the "Big O" isn't *orgasm*—it's *oneness*.

Time spent together in nonsexual interaction is the foundation for improving your sexual experience.

> *Spiritual intimacy is your fuel, emotional intimacy is your gauge, and sexual intimacy is your expression of both.*

If you're struggling to have an intimate, satisfying, and fulfilling sexual relationship with your spouse, examine the order of your intimacy. You may need to apologize to your spouse for your role in starting your sexual intimacy before establishing a solid spiritual and emotional relationship. You may need to apologize for ignoring the impact that a spiritual connection will have on your sex life.

Once your spiritual intimacy and emotional intimacy are thriving, a fulfilling physical and sexual intimacy will be the natural outcome.

🔑 Key Thought:

Your **sexual** relationship with your spouse prospers when your **spiritual** intimacy and **emotional** intimacy flourish.

How has your sexual intimacy flowed from your spiritual and emotional intimacy?

2. BE A GIVER, NOT A TAKER

The husband must fulfill his duty to his wife, and likewise the wife also to her husband. The wife does not have authority over her own body, but the husband does; and likewise, the husband also does not have authority over his own body, but the wife does. (1 Cor. 7:3–4)

This verse has been used in many books and sermons to tell wives they have a "duty" to sexually fulfill their husbands and insinuates if they don't, their husbands are going to cheat. When sex is provided out of any thought of fear, including husbands going elsewhere, the sense of obligation can rob joy from the wife's sexual experience and she foregoes her pleasure, believing sex is all about her husband's fulfillment.

As a result, wives' sexual fulfillment in many marriages has been overlooked or dismissed. Husbands hurry to the main event with little foreplay or waiting for their wives' sexual response.

Few seem to read and understand or acknowledge that the husband's sexual duty to his wife is listed *first* in the verse!

Wives need to become equal participants of joy and pleasure in sexual intimacy and see their sexuality as equally important. Wives should liberally communicate to their husbands what they like and don't like and help their husbands understand they, like their husbands, desire sexual satisfaction. Most men are excited to see their wives enjoying sex, but they struggle to understand what their wives desire in order to become exhilarated in sexual love. Husbands should slow down and listen and wives should communicate, direct, and encourage their husbands to allow her feelings to develop, and gently guide the sexual experience to feel good for both spouses.

Husbands may also believe this verse means they have complete authority over their wives' bodies and that wives must do everything their husbands desire sexually.

Wrong.

A husband may even point out that she's sinning if she refuses to have sex with him.

Wrong.

The above verse says you each have authority over the other's body, but *what authority* do you both have?

You each have the authority to *serve* the other as a *giver* of sexual pleasure—not a taker. The husband and wife "must fulfill" each other by giving, not taking. No one else has this authority over your bodies.

When you become a giver, your spouse can enjoy being a receiver. Marital sex is a beautiful relationship of giving and receiving, with no demands or taking.

When a wife consistently experiences her husband as a giver, she will desire to transfer her authority over her body to her husband. But when she experiences a lust-filled husband, always demanding and taking for his own needs, she pulls back, feeling unprotected, exploited, and devalued.

How did God use His authority over man?

> For God so loved the world, that He *gave* His only Son, so that everyone who believes in Him will not perish, but have eternal life. (John 3:16, emphasis added)

God demonstrated His love for us by *giving* His Son. He didn't use His authority to take from us. The only things God took from us were things that harm and destroy us: the curse of the law of sin and death and our shame. God giving to us is the same picture Jesus portrayed for us:

> The Son of Man did not come to be served, but to serve, and to give His life as a ransom for many. (Matt. 20:28)

Jesus came to serve. He was a giver of life—not a taker.

Within a relationship of love that reflects the character of God, there is only giving—no taking. Therefore, sexual intimacy is about serving your spouse. There should be only givers and receivers in your relationship—no takers.

When both spouses are committed to giving, they eagerly search for ways to please each other and make no demands. They enjoy seeing their spouse receive.

> **Key Thought:**
>
> You have authority over your spouse's body to be a **giver**, not a **taker**.
>
> Have you been a giver or a taker in the bedroom?

3. NO DUTY SEX

Unfortunately, due to humankind skewing God's Word, many husbands believe the wife does not have the authority to say no to sex and must always be available to serve her husband sexually. Consequently, this lie perpetuates many wives engaging in "duty sex."

Duty sex occurs when a giving spouse continues to give sexually when the couple's spiritual and emotional intimacy is low or nonexistent. The giver has duty sex because they fear abandonment or rejection.

Duty sex lacks spiritual and emotional intimacy and cheapens the sexual experience.

The wife typically provides duty sex, and the couple's lack of spiritual and emotional intimacy causes her to feel abandoned, used, dirty, and devalued. She may sense her husband's mind is somewhere else, and she may have dreams or thoughts of spousal infidelity that makes her angry.

When a husband receives duty sex, he senses her lack of engagement, which feels like rejection in his soul. Though he may feel a sexual release, he doesn't feel completely satisfied, no matter how much sex he has, because he isn't experiencing the needed and fulfilling emotional and spiritual connections that will truly satisfy him. Although he may willingly be a taker, he may not be able to describe why sex isn't fully satisfying. So he may frequently turn to porn or other people for sexual satisfaction. But these never satisfy the longing in his soul and spirit. In his frustration, he may demand more frequent sex in the false belief that more will satisfy him. It never does.

> *In searching for true fulfillment,*
> *people pursue sexual activity rather than intimacy.*

Contrary to a husband's desire for more frequent sex, duty sex leads to increasingly lower sexual frequency. Both spouses' bitterness and avoidance of sex increase over time, which expands the gap in their emotional relationship—yet another crazy cycle.

If you're experiencing duty sex in your marriage, you need to discuss this openly with your spouse. It's likely not creating real sexual fulfillment for either of you.

> 🔑 **Key Thought:**
>
> Duty sex will never produce real **spiritual** and **emotional** intimacy that is fully **satisfying**.
>
> What has your experience been with duty sex?

4. YOUR PAST ROBS YOU

> Marriage is to be held in honor among all, and the marriage bed is to be undefiled; for God will judge the sexually immoral and adulterers. (Heb. 13:4)

God designed sex to be completely satisfying between husband and wife. Yet many temptations can lure us from God's plan and dishonor our marriages. So we need to protect our sexual experiences and keep them pure.

What does the verse mean by *honor*? In defining the Greek word *timios* (translated as "honor"), *Strong's Exhaustive Concordance* says we should hold marriage as dear, precious, and valuable.[2] In this context, you can see how fornication and adultery dishonor marriage and defile the marriage bed.

Let's first look at fornication, which is sex before marriage. Sexual immorality, even before marriage, can hurt and defile your sexual intimacy in marriage. Although sex before marriage has become commonplace, very few people believe their marital sex life will be hurt by prior sexual activity (intercourse and sexual experiences short of intercourse).

Sexual experiences before marriage are not limited to prior partners but include pornography, erotic novels, sexually charged movies, and advertising. Any type of premarital sexual experience can consume the thoughts of married couples during their lovemaking. Very few people with prior sexual partners and other experiences will admit to having such thoughts. Nonetheless, these intrusions happen in just about everybody. Thoughts of other partners and sexual scenarios rob sexual intimacy from husbands and wives.

The above verse (Heb. 13:4) also says adultery defiles the marriage bed. Adultery is the sexual immorality of a married man or woman.

Jesus said:

> "Everyone who looks at a woman with lust for her has already committed adultery with her in his heart." (Matt. 5:28)

---

2 Bible Hub, s.v. "timios," accessed March 21, 2022, https://biblehub.com/greek/5093.htm.

Thereby, adultery includes not only a sexual act outside of marriage but also coveting (sexually desiring) anyone other than your spouse.

Desiring others is the root of porn. Pornography sears into your mind the images of others that can frequently resurface when making love to your spouse. Such intrusions make it more difficult to connect with your spouse.

Porn, masturbation, and other sexual lures will cause you to become entirely self-centered, training you to be a taker. Because there is no spiritual or emotional intimacy in sexual lures, users are constantly on a mission to find something to provide more excitement and genuine satisfaction. Impossible. There is no way to have a satisfying sexual relationship with your spouse while thinking about past sexual partners, experiences, and exposures. Not only will you feel the dissatisfaction and guilt inside you, but your spouse will also pick up on these, even in their dreams. Porn, masturbation, and other sexual lures are *real issues* that rob sexual desire and fulfillment from both spouses.

We thank God that He has made provision for sins that "defile the marriage bed," including fornication, adultery, and porn. His healing and His other provisions for us begin with our confession and repentance to Him, our spouses, and others harmed by our sins.

Key Thought:

Sexual immorality before and in marriage is a **robber**.

How has sexual immorality affected sexual intimacy with your spouse?

5. RECEIVE GOD'S HEALING

Flee sexual immorality. Every other sin that a person commits is outside the body, but the sexually immoral person sins against his own body. (1 Cor. 6:18)

According to this verse, sexual immorality is in a unique category as the only sin against a person's *own* body. What does this mean?

Let's revisit ownership: If you steal from your neighbor, you've harmed your neighbor by robbing what belongs to them. But if you commit sexual immorality, you've not only harmed your spouse by robbing what belongs to them but also wounded your body sexually.

With this reminder about ownership, we understand why our spouses are deeply offended when we've been sexually immoral: because your body is shared property with your spouse!

Sexually, what primarily robs us is our past. It must have been great to be Adam and Eve because they had no sexual past. Their lack of experience made them unashamed in their nakedness (like young children). It wasn't until they sinned that their eyes opened to their nakedness, and shame entered. Today, it's rare for someone to enter marriage without a sexual past.

God wants to free you from the oppression of your past. But to receive freedom, you must be open and honest about your past—what happened to you and what you've done against others that dishonored them, yourself, and God.

For some, honesty may include things you persuaded your spouse to do sexually before and after marriage. Honesty may also include confessing your adultery and lust that was driven by porn, sexual chat rooms, or erotic romance novels.

Honesty, openness, transparency, and humility position you to receive God's grace that will free and heal you from your past wounds and give you new life.

> *As you expose past sexual sins that dominate your thinking, they will lose their power over you.*

Becoming HOT about your sexual wounds is where healing starts. Going to God and your spouse with your wounds may feel awkward, but He already knows what's going on in your heart. He wants you to come out of secrecy and openly give your wounds to Him to heal and restore your spirit and relationship with your spouse.

God can enable you to enjoy a sexual relationship with your spouse and be fully satisfied without thinking of others, whether real or imagined. God has His riches in store for you—His best for you, your spouse, and your sexual relationship together.

Key Thought:

God wants to **heal** your sexual wounds so you can **enjoy** sexual intimacy with your spouse.

How do you feel about asking God to heal your sexual wounds?

6. INVITE THE HOLY SPIRIT TO BE YOUR TEACHER

> I have come into my garden, my sister, my bride; I have gathered my myrrh along with my balsam. I have eaten my honeycomb with my honey; I have drunk my wine with my milk. Eat, friends; Drink and drink deeply, lovers. (Song of Sol. 5:1)

The book of Song of Solomon portrays an intimate relationship between a Shulamite woman and her lover (who some say was King Solomon). The last sentence of the verse is God talking to the happy couple, encouraging them to "drink and drink deeply." Some translations even say they should be drunk with love (ESV).

Generally, sex is known as lovemaking. However, we prefer *lovesharing*. When you enjoy sexual intimacy with your spouse, you have the opportunity to physically express and share the love you're already sharing in your spirit and soul. You aren't making love but sharing it.

Of course, if you haven't experienced the love of God in your spirit and soul, you have nothing to share with your spouse except an animalistic, lustful desire for sex. This description is what sex typically is for people who have no spiritual and emotional connection and explains why sex between strangers is common (hookups).

In the Garden of Eden, God was with Adam and Eve, teaching them about His wonderful creation of sex, and they were open to His teaching. The sexual lovesharing between Adam and Eve was completely pure, and they thought it was normal to have God present with them while they shared their love. In the same way, His Holy Spirit is available to teach us about sexual fulfillment with our spouses. We need to mirror Adam and Eve's openness to God and draw insight from the sexual lovesharing in Song of Solomon.

Most couples have a routine sexual experience; partners know the steps before they happen. But when you, as a couple, ask God to improve your sexual experience and embrace Him in your sexual union, expect things to change for the better. God, the Creator of sexual pleasure, wants to be your sexual guide rather than media and porn.

How do you embrace God during lovesharing? Begin with prayer before sex, welcoming God's presence and His direction into your time together. Ask God to make your thoughts focused only on each other. Ask Him to show you where to place your hands, how to touch each other, and the pace and pressure.

Sex is God's gift of physical intimacy and enjoyment and a way to express His love to each other in marriage. God wants you to be intoxicated with lovesharing, like the Shulamite woman and her lover. Sexual intimacy and its physical, emotional, and spiritual fulfillments are blessings from God. To experience these blessings, look to the Holy Spirit to be your teacher. He will "guide you into *all* the truth" (John 16:13, emphasis added).

When the Bible says *all*, it means *all*—including the truth about sex. Even though we intellectually believe that the Holy Spirit is with us wherever we go, we think this includes everywhere *except the bedroom*!

One thing the Holy Spirit may lead you to do is change the atmosphere of your bedroom. How can your room be set up to create the most inviting and exciting environment for lovesharing? What can you both do to make the ambiance more enticing for each other? How can you create an environment that affects all five senses?

During your lovesharing experience, your five senses should come alive in unique ways. Song of Solomon is an excellent reference, as the book intimately describes the use of all five senses in physical intimacy.

1. Sight: You can experience physical intimacy through what you see.

Sight is a very important part of sex, especially for those who are visually stimulated. Sight is important, not only for arousal but for intensifying the lasting impact of lovesharing. Keep enough light on in the room to see each other. Try candles. Light them every night, even if the time has been committed to just talking.

Sex in the dark can more easily encourage your mind to wander back to past sexual sin experiences, especially for spouses who've had numerous past sexual partners or had been using porn. While turning on some lights will not necessarily fix the past, this change is another means to create new memories.

Physiologically, whatever you see during orgasm imprints on your mind, especially for men. The next time you and your spouse are lovesharing, be intentional about looking into each other's eyes during orgasm. The more you connect visually with your spouse, the more you'll become attached to your climax, which is why porn is so enticing but harmful. After repeated orgasms to porn, your view of what's most exciting becomes porn images rather than your spouse. Imprints of porn sometimes lead to erectile dysfunction and the desire to include porn as part of the sexual experience with spouses.

In "Becoming a Sexually Successful Man," author Douglas Weiss (*Sex, Men and God*) shares the fracturing of the brain that occurs when we're experiencing orgasms while focused on anything other than our spouse. He calls this fracturing a "dual or multi-focused brain."[3] An individual whose brain is psychologically fractured believes the world is all about meeting their needs. They're typically disconnected emotionally from their spouses and discontented with their sex life.

When your brain is focused solely on sexual experiences with your spouse, your brain is uni-focused: there are no distractions.

The amazing thing is that a person with a uni-focused brain experiences stronger and more satisfying orgasms with their spouse than those with dual- or multifocused brains.

A dual- or multifocused brain can be retrained to uni-focused by making your spouse your exclusive sexual experience, both physically and mentally. You become aroused by how you allow yourself to become aroused. When your spouse is your exclusive sexual stimulation, that's what becomes satisfying over time.

2. Smell: You can experience intimacy through what you smell.

Smell has an amazing ability to help us remember things from our past. Have you ever smelled something and remembered a particular place and time? Try using incense, oil diffusers, candles, perfumes, and other smells that set the mood for your uni-focused sexual intimacy. When you begin to associate the smells with uni-focused lovesharing, you'll anticipate your lovesharing times. Those familiar aromas can also be a beautiful signal when a spouse shows up in bed with the familiar scent.

3. Taste: You can experience intimacy through what you taste.

Your mouth is full of sensory perception. Kissing can be sweet-tasting, and God wants you to use your sense of taste with your spouse in lovesharing. Song of Solomon is full of erotic descriptions using taste. You can incorporate foods in your lovesharing. There's no way to experience taste without using your mouth and tongue, and God can use these to cultivate wonderful sexual feelings.

4. Hearing: You can experience intimacy through what you hear.

Hearing is multifaceted. Beautiful music or sounds can set a lovesharing atmosphere. Try listening to instrumental worship music when you're together.

---

[3] Doug Weiss, "Becoming A Sexually Successful Man," Medium, June 1, 2018, https://medium.com/drdougweiss/becoming-a-sexually-successful-man-f94affdfbd9d.

Pay attention to the sounds and words that come from each other. Your words can create a beautiful atmosphere.

The first place a man needs to learn to loveshare with his wife is between her ears. You may have heard people say the brain is the most important sex organ. Engage your spouse through beautiful, tender, caring words during sexual intimacy—not crass words that porn actors use.

5. Touch: You can experience intimacy through the way you touch.

Touch is naturally essential to lovesharing. However, unfortunately, too many couples rely solely on touch. Ask God to show you a new way to touch your spouse, a symbolic touch from God that flows through your bodies to each other.

Women typically enjoy nonsexual touching to begin lovesharing and generally like a lighter touch than men. For example, circle patterns are more pleasurable than just stroking, and slower is more pleasing than faster.

In media (especially porn), women are portrayed as enjoying "rough sex." However, many women want exactly the opposite. Rough sex is demoralizing and objectifying to women.

Men, ask your wives about their touch preference regarding your lovesharing. Once you stop looking at porn, you will no longer continually desire what you've seen. Remember that you are aroused by whatever you allow yourself to be aroused by, including rough sex.

Experiencing all five senses in your lovesharing might seem like a lot to think about, so consider that everyone likes to have times of being treated as special and feeling special. You might not eat at the grand buffet for every meal, but it's especially nice on occasion. And once you're used to the grand buffet, you may no longer want to have the continental breakfast!

Here's another interesting thought about using your five senses. When God designed the tabernacle in the wilderness for the Israelites to use as their traveling temple, He designated a room He called the Holy of Holies where He would show up over the mercy seat. It was a place of intimacy between the high priest and God.

In designing the Holy of Holies as a special place of spiritual intimacy, God also created a five-senses experience! He directed Moses that the room have candles to see, incense to smell, water to bathe in (touch), bread to eat, and, later in the temple, music to hear. God set the five-senses pattern to help the priest fully experience intimacy with Him, which is an example of how we can fully enjoy intimacy with our spouses. So the next time you're planning an evening of lovesharing, think about how you can create your own tabernacle experience!

Consider these thoughts:

- Have you ever prayed as a couple about your sexual relationship? If not, what do you want God to do for you?
- Do you believe the Holy Spirit can lead you and your spouse to enjoy a sexual relationship that's completely satisfying and fulfilling? God is not only able; He's eager to help you. Invite Him into your next sexual experience as husband and wife.

> 🔑 **Key Thought:**
>
> Ask the Holy Spirit to **teach** you how to enjoy sex that connects you **emotionally** and **spiritually** to your spouse.
>
> How do you feel about inviting the Holy Spirit into your sexual experience?

7. WAITING IS IMPORTANT

> Those who wait for the Lord will gain new strength; they will mount up with wings like eagles, they will run and not get tired, they will walk and not become weary. (Isa. 40:31)
>
> I wait for the Lord, my soul waits, and I wait for His word. (Ps. 130:5)

Waiting is important to our relationships with God and important in our sexual relationship with our spouse.

The first point of waiting should have been before marriage, but frequently, even those who waited for marriage to have intercourse let themselves enjoy other sexual activities before marriage. So most couples started a pattern of not waiting that continued into their marriages: impatience with each other during sexual intimacy and unwillingness to wait for each other to try new experiences.

Many men want their wives to be more sexually aggressive, but before and during lovesharing, they don't wait for her readiness. They aggressively take from her before she offers. When a wife feels that her husband is a taker and not a giver, her innate protection kicks in, and she begins to shut down and becomes reluctant to offer herself.

Husbands, if movies have set your expectations for sex (people jumping into bed with little prelude), you may not be providing adequate time for your wife to warm up. Once you begin the practice of waiting on her response, you may see more sexual aggressiveness. But you'll need to learn to wait! Women just take longer to feel sexual arousal than men. Perhaps this God-designed difference was to help men learn the importance of patience and being attentive to their wives.

When a husband decides to wait for his wife's sexual response, he's giving her time to become ready. Waiting is a way for the husband to be a giver. He shows her that it's more important to wait for her readiness to offer herself than for him to take from her before she's ready. Waiting enables the wife to feel pleasure in offering herself to her husband and produces a sexual experience that's fully pleasurable for her and her husband.

In fulfilling our sexual desires, we also have to recognize limits based on what our spouses mutually desire to experience with us. For men especially (but not exclusively), sexual desires without limits can encompass all sorts of fantasies that cause us to focus on ourselves rather than our spouse. We need to see our spouse's limits as God-given for our good.

We can become frustrated with limits, always wanting more, and allow bitterness and disappointment to become our pass card to find other sexual experiences. Instead, we should turn to God with our desires, asking Him to teach us sexual experiences that are mutually enjoyable. God is the Creator of sex. In Him, we can enjoy sexual experiences to their fullest potential within those mutually agreed-upon perimeters.

Waiting also means not rushing toward orgasm. Waiting brings strength to the sexual response. The more you enjoy the teasing and foreplay, the stronger the reward.

Lingering at the finish is another way to wait. Women take a long time to warm up and cool down. They want to feel cherished and appreciated at the end. So, men: After sex, don't rush off or go to sleep! Cherish your wife by lingering and using words that express closeness and appreciation.

Talk with your spouse about waiting. Ask for an honest response about the pace of your lovesharing, and receive the response with humility and thankfulness. Let your spouse set the pace the next time you're intimate.

> Stop depriving one another, except by agreement for a time so that you may devote yourselves to prayer, and come together again so that Satan will not tempt you because of your lack of self-control. (1 Cor. 7:5)

In sexuality, you may need to have a time of sexual fasting with prayer to address your sexual issues, asking God to heal your sexual problems. Abstaining from sex for prayer about your sex life is very powerful. Prayer and fasting sex can do amazing things for your desire. Note that the verse even infers you and your spouse should reunite sexually because your desire can be so strong that it will be hard to control.

God doesn't require us to sexually fast, but if you're experiencing significant sexual problems, consider a sexual fast for prayer, and ask God to heal you.

🔑 Key Thought:

Waiting can help your sexual intimacy grow **stronger**.

How should you have waited in the past? What can you change going forward?

After the group session, turn to Appendix A and complete your Two-Minute Takeaway.

Session 8: Homework Assignment

1. Complete the Sexual Behaviors and Feelings Inventory on the next page. Ask the Holy Spirit to show you whether there is anything in your sexual history contributing to your current problems, either spiritually, emotionally, or sexually. Record those below.

   _____
   _____
   _____
   _____

2. Evaluate whether you're a giver in your sexual relationship. Identify things you need to change to show your spouse that you're a giver, and record those here.

   _____
   _____
   _____
   _____

3. Share your answers from 1 and 2 above with your spouse, and ask for their input. Remember not to be defensive or blame your spouse. Be humble, empathetic, and compassionate. Record your most significant issues, needs, and desires below. Pray together, and seek God's healing.

   _____
   _____
   _____
   _____

4. Discuss with your spouse how the atmosphere around your intimacy should change to invite God into your sexual experience. What do you want God to do for you? Record your thoughts below. Pray together, and ask God to make His presence known when you approach intimate moments with each other.

   _____
   _____
   _____
   _____

5. Share your Two-Minute Takeaway, and record in Appendix A your agreed-upon action steps.

ACTIVITY: SEXUAL BEHAVIORS AND FEELINGS INVENTORY

1. Review the following list of sexual behaviors and feelings, and rate the frequency at which you've experienced these using the following scale.

2. For ratings of 5 or higher, describe how those affect your sexual relationship, and ask God to help you remember how, when, and why those issues started. The following behaviors and feelings can frequently impact your sexual relationship negatively.

   9: Completely or extremely
   8: Strongly (almost always)
   7: A great deal
   6: Very much
   5: A fair amount
   4: Somewhat (not often)
   3: Slightly
   2: Very little
   1: Not at all

No.	Sexual Behavior or Feeling	Rating	Impact on your sex life—how, when, and why did this start?
1	Low desire		
2	Comparison to past sexual partners		
3	Feeling used for sex or feeling dirty		
4	Sex as an obligation, duty, or service		
5	Preoccupation with sexual fantasies		
6	Viewing pornography or other sensual material		
7	Long periods of celibacy		
8	Alcohol, drugs		
9	Lack of time		
10	Hormones		
11	Exhaustion		
12	No orgasms		

SESSION 8: BECOMING A GIVER, NOT A TAKER • 129

No.	Sexual Behavior or Feeling	Rating	Impact on your sex life—how, when, and why did this start?
13	Lack of arousal		
14	Poor emotional self-image		
15	Poor body self-image		
16	Depression		
17	Boredom, routine		
18	Fear		
19	Physical pain		
20	Lack of privacy		
21	Sexual-performance pressure		
22	Disagreements on frequency		
23	Repeated sexual frustration		
24	Thoughts of infidelity		
25	Thoughts of a past abortion		
26	Recurring thoughts from previous sexual experiences of direct physical contact		
27	Inhibition/lies caused by spouse's previous experiences		
28	Thoughts of past sexual trauma or abuse		
29	Wrong views about sex from upbringing		
30	Homosexual experiences or feelings		
31	Masturbation		
32	Wound collecting/unforgiveness		
33	Bitterness, anger, contempt for your spouse		
34	No cherishing or love from spouse		

No.	Sexual Behavior or Feeling	Rating	Impact on your sex life—how, when, and why did this start?
35	No respect from spouse		
36	Busyness and stress		
37	Secret sexual sins hidden from spouse		
38	Flirting with others		
39	Thoughts of other sexual experiences of nondirect physical contact (strip clubs, phone sex, etc.)		
40	Convincing spouse or forcing unwanted sexual behaviors onto spouse		
41	Being convinced or forced into unwanted sexual behaviors by spouse		
42	Placing your job or family in jeopardy to receive sexual favors		
43	Paying money for sexual gratification		
44	Secret online identity to search out sexual sites		
45	Hidden online activities		
46	Using pornography with spouse to "enhance" experience		
47	Sexual fantasies to achieve arousal or orgasm		
48	Anxiety that sexual behaviors will be discovered		
49	Hurting or being hurt emotionally/physically during sex		
50	Sexual desire that is more than you can control		
51	Viewing or experiencing sexual activities with minors or animals		
52	Thoughts of incest as the perpetrator or victim		
53	Sense of emotional or sexual betrayal by spouse		
54	Soul ties to previous sexual or emotional relationships		
55	Anxiety about poor sexual performance		

Notes

SESSION 9:
BECOMING BATTLE PARTNERS

Excerpt from *Savage Marriage*

Priscilla

Six months had passed since Phil came clean, and we attended a Couples Weekend Intensive with Whatever It Takes Ministries. At one point, Jenny Speed asked each attendant to face their spouse and say, "You're not my enemy."

As Phil and I did that and embraced, there was a glimmer in our eyes as we felt new emotions of togetherness and realized we had come a long way in six months. Gone was the fear that we would have to live in this mess for five to ten years before God would heal us. Gone was our old life of hypocrisy, chasing a pretend Christianity while wallowing in depression and anxiety that sucked the life from us. Gone were the anger and bitterness that had dominated my life. And gone was the unforgiveness that had demanded revenge on Phil.

We were not enemies; we were battle partners.

For the first time in our marriage, we were engaging in an epic quest for life together—a new season, a new chapter without secrets. The shame and wounds of our past were behind us, and it was time to rebuild, to create a new relationship.

Congratulations! You've made it to the final session: Becoming Battle Partners! This session will provide the foundation for you to move from Savage Marriage with the confidence that you can overcome your past and fight for your future.

1. EMBRACE COMPANIONSHIP

> Then the Lord God said, "It is not good for the man to be alone; I will make him a helper suitable for him." (Gen. 2:18)

God's first purpose for Eve wasn't procreation—it was companionship.

Think about your spouse. Why did you marry? What purpose did you believe your spouse would fulfill in your life?

When couples first meet, they typically look for a companion who's emotionally engaging and sexually attractive, and they can't seem to spend enough time together. Everything else in life takes a back seat to their relationship, and a physical touch generates smiles and tingles.

After a few years of marriage, *fun* and *sexy* make room for other values, such as financial stability, good parenting, and running the family home. Couples learn that with bills to pay and crying kids to feed, it's hard to be consistently fun and sexy.

Managing a home and family is a lot of work, and the original goal of a fun and sexy companionship fades. Work, hobbies, and friends also consume time, and many spouses feel isolated and lonely, though others are around. Then they look for someone else to be their companion.

> *Just because you're married doesn't mean you're showing companionship to your spouse.*

Some spouses feel like they're simply roommates. Others feel that work schedules, travel, kids' activities, appointments, and other to-dos take up all the time, and there's simply none left for Mom and Dad as spousal companions. Often a couple's communication style through the years becomes so combative they stay out of each other's way.

If any portion of this sounds like your marriage, your spouse is at risk of looking elsewhere for companionship. The circumstances do not justify adultery but do explain the emotional factors of why adultery happens. Remember that adultery isn't exclusive to acts of sex but also includes sexual thoughts of others and emotional betrayal. While a spouse may not have a sexual affair, they could develop a relationship with someone else, which steals marital intimacy.

BECOMING BATTLE PARTNERS

The first step in becoming battle partners is to seriously consider your time spent together. True companionship with your spouse means prioritizing time together—not for sex alone but for spiritual and emotional bonding, which includes nonsexual fun together.

Making time for true companionship may mean changing your job, letting go of a hobby, and restructuring anything else that will help place your spouse first. If you aren't willing to at least be a companion to your spouse, there's no way you can ever achieve true intimacy, much less become battle partners.

Key Thought:

You must be a **companion** before you can be a battle partner.

What needs to change for you to be a better companion to your spouse?

2. NO DIVIDED HOUSE

> Two are better than one because they have a good return for their labor: for if either of them falls, the one will lift up his companion. But woe to the one who falls when there is not another to lift him up! Furthermore, if two lie down together they keep warm, but how can one be warm alone? And if one can overpower him who is alone, two can resist him. A cord of three strands is not quickly torn apart. (Eccl. 4:9–12)

What do you do when you encounter problems you can't handle on your own?

Many people turn to counselors, accountability partners or groups, and surveillance devices to control addictions. Few people turn to their spouses. While they may confide in their spouse, that's different than asking and believing their spouse can truly help them.

Your spouse has more at stake in your healing than anyone else. When you bury your pride and humbly ask your spouse for help, you trigger a God-given desire inside them that's difficult for them to resist. Their encouragement, compassion, and insight can help create freedom and healing that you'll never achieve through any other efforts.

The enemy wants to divide spousal relationships, and he accomplishes this when our battles become individual, internal, private fights. Remember that the serpent tried to divide Adam and Eve's relationship in the garden. Adam told God that Eve was to blame. We've seen how the serpent has successfully divided couples from the beginning of time. He got Adam and Eve to be on opposite sides of the battle. They began to battle each other rather than be battle partners against the serpent.

> *You can never be a partner with someone you see as your enemy.*

Be on guard: The devil's biggest strategy is to divide your marriage. If he convinces you that your spouse is your enemy, he's successfully created a divided house—a compromised structure more susceptible to collapsing and injuring you and your family.

In Mark 3, the Pharisees accused Jesus of casting out demons by using power from the devil. Jesus replied with logic and truth, "How can Satan cast out Satan? . . . If a house is divided against itself, that house will not be able to stand" (Mark 3:23–25).

If you've allowed your marriage to become a divided house, the journey to victory will be long and hard—"but with God all things are possible" (Matt. 19:26). God is on your side (Ps. 46:7), and "greater is He who is in you than he who is in the world" (1 John 4:4).

We are all in a spiritual battle. But the truth is that the battle is not with our spouses but with the enemy of our souls. When you feel like your spouse is your enemy, you have to renounce such lies as Jesus did and ask God to help you stand united as battle partners. God's plan for your marriage is victory, and He is in the battle with you, making a way where there seems to be no way (Isa. 43:19).

> ### 🔑 Key Thought:
>
> To become battle partners, you must believe you are **stronger** when your **spouse** helps fight your battles.
>
> Look each other in the eyes and say, "You are not my enemy." How did this make you feel? How has "being an enemy" been a problem in your marriage?

3. TRANSFORM CRITICISM INTO COMPASSIONATE ENCOURAGEMENT

"How can you say to your brother, 'Brother, let me take out the speck that is in your eye,' when you yourself do not see the log that is in your own eye? You hypocrite, first take the log out of your own eye, and then you will see clearly to take out the speck that is in your brother's eye." (Luke 6:42)

Having a trusted friend (such as your spouse) point out a "speck in your eye" is valuable because others see blind spots you cannot see. However, before you return the favor (showing what's wrong in their lives), you must be willing to listen, see, and then describe to them what's wrong in your life. Such introspection and confession take humility.

Be aware and cautious of your tongue and attitude. When you speak like you have a gift of criticism, you're playing into the enemy's house-dividing plan because no such gift is among the gifts of the Holy Spirit. When used as God intended, His gifts to us will build up others, not tear them down, and produce the fruit of the Spirit.

Do not turn your freedom into an opportunity for the flesh, but serve one another through love. (Gal. 5:13)

The critical person feels superior when pointing out what's wrong in someone else's life because their spirit is rooted in and consumed with pride, leaving the other person feeling torn down.

To be a battle partner with your spouse, you must humbly renew your thinking and change your communication style if your tendency is criticism. Anytime you're inclined to point out a wrong or weakness in your spouse, start by admitting something you need to change in yourself that's in a similar vein. Show compassion to your spouse about a weakness you see in them while encouraging them that with God's help, you both can do better and be stronger allies together.

When you become consumed by your spouse's problems and shortcomings, ask the Holy Spirit to help you see and reflect on *your* issues—beginning with your pride. What else do you need to change in yourself? How have you contributed to the current conflict?

Even when you're only 10 percent responsible for a conflict, you need to own 100 percent of your 10 percent out loud to your spouse. Taking responsibility for your part and problems will open a path to mutual reconciliation and allow you to be an effective battle partner for and with your spouse.

> 🔑 **Key Thought:**
>
> Your **critical** spirit will **destroy** your opportunity to be a battle partner.
>
> What role does criticism play in your marriage?

ACTIVITY:

For items 4 and 5, rate what you can do to help your spouse become your battle partner, and rate the things you can do to become your spouse's battle partner. In other words, being allies is a two-way street; both spouses must be willing to embrace the other as a battle partner to effectively protect your marriage.

After each statement, use the following scale to rate how well *you* are doing in each area. You'll use this in your homework assignment.

9: Completely or extremely
8: Strongly (almost always)
7: A great deal
6: Very much
5: A fair amount
4: Somewhat (not often)
3: Slightly
2: Very little
1: Not at all

4. ENCOURAGING YOUR SPOUSE TO BE YOUR BATTLE PARTNER

1) Be transparent about your weaknesses.

> Each one is tempted when he is carried away and enticed by his own lust. Then when lust has conceived, it gives birth to sin; and sin, when it has run its course, brings forth death. (James 1:14–15)

A woman on the board of a charitable organization died suddenly in her forties. The email announcing her death said she had lost her private battle with cancer. She had worked side by side with her fellow board members and had not let anyone know about her sickness and need for help. She died without anyone helping her bear her burden.

Our pride can keep us from sharing our weaknesses with our spouses because we want to appear strong, and we may not want to be "a burden," even when we have all sorts of internal conflicts.

To be an effective battle partner and encourage your spouse to join your battles, you must be honest, open, and transparent about your weaknesses. This doesn't mean limiting your openness to your general weaknesses or sharing only when you believe sin is inevitable. Sharing your thoughts and feelings also means identifying trigger points that lead to sin and involving your spouse when you encounter a trigger point.

> *Sin doesn't occur randomly.*
> *It has a life cycle of conception, birth, and growth.*

If you study your patterns of sin, you may see trigger points and ritualistic behaviors that happen even months before you act out. Sometimes a counselor will ask questions to help you identify trigger points. Sometimes you (or your spouse) will already know them. Either way, once you see a pattern emerging that inevitably leads to sin, you must immediately involve your spouse. An infantryman never goes into battle alone, just as Jesus never sent His disciples out alone but in pairs.

> *Bringing the sin you're contemplating out of the darkness,*
> *into the light, has the power to break your cycle of sin.*

When you reveal your weaknesses to your spouse, they feel needed and valued as your battle partner. Being vulnerable has the power to move your relationship deeper into emotional intimacy and trust and helps you maintain your place on the low and narrow road of humility and transparency.

Your rating: _____

2) Be accountable to your spouse regarding your progress.

Our pride tells us we can handle it all and need to keep our battles secret. But humility says we become accountable to our spouses because our sin affects them.

We seek and pay doctors and counselors for help not only due to their training but because they aren't personally affected by our problems. God can use our spouses in a much different way because they love us and have a personal stake in our healing. A spouse's humility, empathy, and compassion can provide far more encouragement than paid professionals. We're not saying you shouldn't seek professionals, but you should be HOT and accountable with your spouse.

For example, when you're battling sexual temptation, send a text to your spouse with the praying-hands emoji. This tool can be a code that informs your spouse that you're in the middle of a mental battle and need help.

A meaningful response from your spouse can provide strength to overcome temptation. You'll immediately feel relief because your temptation is no longer a secret and you will sense the strength of your battle partner standing with you.

Later in the day, when you're face to face, your spouse can ask why you sent the text, or better yet, you can volunteer the story. Either way, you can explain from a place of victory.

> *Self-disclosure allows you to take your thoughts fully captive.*

For though we walk in the flesh, we do not wage battle according to the flesh, for the weapons of our warfare are not of the flesh, but divinely powerful for the destruction of fortresses. We are destroying arguments and all arrogance raised against the knowledge of God, and we are taking every thought captive to the obedience of Christ. (2 Cor. 10:3–5)

If you choose to fight the mental battle alone rather than partner with your spouse in battle, your thoughts will take you captive. When you bring your thoughts out of darkness, into the light, by revealing them, you're taking your thoughts captive to the obedience of Christ.

Talk with your spouse about trying the text-code method of engaging as battle partners. Or discuss what other notification means is mutually agreeable. Then institute the system. Consider a method that will not be unduly disruptive to your spouse's responsibilities (such as their job), remembering you simply want to alert them to your situation for prayer, and you can later discuss the details—and from a place of victory.

Remember, the key is to notify your spouse when you first feel the temptation. If you wait until you're deeper in darkness, it's harder to find the light to climb out. And if you wait until after you've already sinned, you're back to square one, making your spouse a confession partner, not a battle partner.

You'll be amazed at how much power you feel to overcome temptation when you immediately ask for your spouse's help as soon as a temptation enters your mind.

Your rating: _____

3) Let your spouse know you need, appreciate, and value their love and assistance.

If you want your spouse to feel like your true battle partner and take ownership in that vital role, praise them for every step they take toward helping you. Let them know you value and respect their opinions, prayers, concern, and responses to your signals for help. Tell them that their support is key to your healing and that you can't win the battles without them.

Remember to avoid being defensive or critical of their suggestions, recognizing that your spouse is trying to help you as your battle partner. Criticism kills the desire to help.

Your rating: _____

5. ENCOURAGING YOUR SPOUSE TO LET YOU BECOME THEIR BATTLE PARTNER

1) Show empathy and compassion in the battles your spouse is fighting.

Remember that empathy and compassion are the doorways to emotional intimacy; it's impossible to be effective battle partners without being emotionally intimate. Empathy and compassion encourage your spouse to trust you. These responses show your spouse that you truly care about them.

The opposite of empathy is apathy. When your spouse shares their struggle and you appear apathetic by minimizing or dismissing their struggle, such as by telling them they should just get over it, don't expect them to share that struggle again! You've shut that door.

Your empathy and compassion toward your spouse, even when you don't understand why they're struggling or can't just stop the behavior, are key to becoming their battle partner.

Your rating: _____

2) Remind your spouse that they have authority over all the enemy's power.

> I have given you the authority to trample on snakes and scorpions, and authority over all the power of the enemy, and nothing will injure you. (Luke 10:19)

The easiest thing to forget in the middle of a spiritual battle is that you have spiritual authority over *every* power and scheme of the enemy. When we focus on the size of our battles, we sometimes need help from someone to remind us that we can take authority over the enemy in the name of Jesus. Your spouse's encouragement can move you out of the battle and into victory.

Your rating: _____

3) Remind and encourage your spouse that they're an overcomer.

> Encourage one another every day, as long as it is still called "today," so that none of you will be hardened by the deceitfulness of sin. (Heb. 3:13)

Trials and conflicts sometimes seem like they'll never end. This feeling can lead to depression or other pits you can't climb out of.

When struggling with a trial, we need someone to tell us we have what it takes to overcome. We need someone who'll remind us that the trial won't last forever and that God is our victorious warrior and rescuer who always has good things planned for us. We each need to hear these words of life in our battles.

When you encourage your spouse with powerful truths, they'll love having you as their battle partner. Rarely does a person reject encouragement when it's presented with genuine care, concern, and humility.

Your rating: _____

4) Help your spouse see the lies of the devil.

> You are of your father the devil, and you want to do the desires of your father. He was a murderer from the beginning, and does not stand in the truth because there is no truth in him. Whenever he tells a lie, he speaks from his own nature, because he is a liar and the father of lies. (John 8:44)

> Be of sober spirit, be on the alert. Your adversary, the devil, prowls around like a roaring lion, seeking someone to devour. (1 Peter 5:8)

When you're listening to the devil's lies in the middle of your struggles, asking your spouse a simple question can illuminate the lies. For example, "What are you hearing?" By your spouse asking that simple question, you'll likely immediately know what lies you're hearing. Once you can then describe the lies, your spouse can help redirect you to the truth.

Your rating: _____

5) Pray with your spouse.

When you're enjoying true spiritual and emotional oneness, your prayers will provide more encouragement than anyone else's because you've joined your spouse in their pain. You feel compassion for their situation, and you laugh and cry with them. Your spouse experiencing your emotional engagement will give them confidence that God is moving.

Offering to pray for your spouse in the middle of their struggle can be powerful and encouraging. To be an effective battle partner, you must learn to pray together. Here are some powerful tools:

- Pray out loud.
- Embrace tears with your prayers if God so opens your emotions.
- Provide meaningful physical touch to your spouse while you're praying.
- Allow opportunity for them to pray with you, but don't insist they pray.

These tools can create tremendous spiritual and emotional unity and victory over the battle (James 5:16). There is no better way to invite God's presence into the middle of your conflicts and struggles.

Your rating: _____

After the group session, turn to Appendix A and complete your Two-Minute Takeaway.

Session 9: Homework Assignment

1. Discuss with your spouse your ratings of items 4 and 5. Ask for their input on whether your self-ratings align with how they see you. Identify areas in yourself that need change, and record them below.

   _____
   _____
   _____

2. Share with your spouse where you need the most help fighting your spiritual battles and where you need encouragement. Record those areas below.

   _____
   _____
   _____

3. Every new journey starts with an initial step. Pray together, and commit to being battle partners.

4. Discuss how you and your spouse can let each other know when a spiritual, emotional, or physical battle is looming, and record below your agreed-upon method. Over the next week, ask your spouse if they've encountered any battles, and determine whether you followed through on letting each other know.

   _____
   _____
   _____

5. Review your Two-Minute Takeaways and homework assignments from the entire *Savage Marriage Study Guide*, and record your top three action items below.

   a. _____

   b. _____

   c. _____

6. Use the template following this homework to write your New Identify Statement. First, read the following example statements for some ideas. Then consider the Preparation Thoughts given after the examples. During our final meeting, you'll have an opportunity to read your New Identity Statement aloud.

Example Identity Statements

I am Jenny Lynne Speed, a beautiful, passionate woman of God who loves God and desires to please Him. I have been called and anointed to exhort others to walk in freedom from sin and pursue righteousness. I speak with wisdom upon my tongue and kindness upon my lips. My trust is in the Lord my God, my Savior, and my deliverer. He protects me, pursues me, and provides for all my needs. I am not alone! He has chosen me because He loves me, and as a result, I am enamored by His love!

I, Wendy, am a precious, valuable, and blessed princess of the King. I am a beautiful creation and enough in my Father's eyes. I am a loyal light-bearer of Christ Jesus, created in His image to be a reflection of Him. In Christ, I am more than a conqueror. Because Jesus shed His blood for me, I am redeemed and qualified to do the work He specifically placed before me. I am chosen and appointed by Jesus to bear His fruit. I have been given the mind of Christ, and I am brave because of Him. I am loved with an everlasting love! Let go, my soul, and trust in Him! Through it all, my eyes are on You, and it is well with me.

I, Doug, am no longer hiding in the shadows. I will no longer conceal my sin by hiding my guilt in my heart. I will no longer fear the crowd and dread their contempt. I will no longer believe the lies from the enemy or his messengers. I will look to the freedom and treasures that are found in Your scars. I will look to the power and truth that waits in Your blood. There is a treasure ahead for me. There are plans for me beyond my last breath. What evil and death I have escaped through fear of You. I am loved with an everlasting love.

I am Phil, the son of a Father whose name is Faithful and True. I bear the imprint of His character in my body, soul, and spirit and seek to experience His truth in my innermost being. I celebrate His faithfulness in my relationships with my wife and family and embrace humility to break the chains of sin and set the captives free. I know God, hear His voice, and follow and obey Him even when the cost is great. I trust God for His victory in my life and proclaim the favorable year of the Lord for my children, my children's children, and the generations to come.

I am Priscilla, the daughter of the Eternal One. He has given me the power and authority to overcome the evil one in my life, to proclaim His goodness to those around me, to heal the brokenhearted, and to restore families with His truth. I will fight valiantly like Deborah to see the goodness of God restored in my family's lives.

I am Chelsea, a beloved daughter of God. From the beginning, God planned to bring me into this world to be a blessing to my family and the people around me. I love to meet peoples' needs, speak truth into their lives, and empower them to pursue their purpose in life. When I serve others, I fully rely on God and trust Him to bear the fruit of His work. When I depend on Him, He does not view me as a burden. In fact, He rejoices that He can hold my hand and walk with me through all areas of my life.

I am Michael, a brave, free bringer of peace. I'm no longer defined by my past sin and failures but by what Christ had done for me. I no longer cower and bend to the lies Satan has told me. I will seek out those who are lost and hurting. I will bring them comfort, encouragement, and grace. I will help bring reconciliation and peace to relationships around me. I am no longer a child but a man who will love and serve his wife and family. I'm not naked and afraid. I'm clothed by God, and I wear the shoes of peace and wield the sword of the Spirit. The gates and plans of hell will not prevail against me.

Statements used by permission.

Preparation Thoughts

While there is no formula for writing your New Identity Statement, here are important preparation thoughts.

1. Ask God to show you who you are in His eyes, and listen to the Holy Spirit's response.

2. Contemplate what God has shown you through Savage Marriage:

    - Who are you?
    - How do you want to reflect God's character?
    - What can you trust Him to do in your life?
    - How do you want others to see you?

3. Share on the statement page how God sees you and how He wants you to see yourself based on everything you've learned over the past nine sessions.

4. Begin your statement with "I am" . . .

My New Identity Statement

Notes

APPENDIX A:
TWO-MINUTE TAKEAWAYS AND ACTION PLANS

SESSION 1: THE TWO ROADS

Two-Minute Takeaway (completed during session): _____
_____
_____

Observation from discussion with spouse (homework): _____
_____
_____

Action step—what God revealed that you need to contemplate or do (homework): _____
_____
_____

SESSION 2: WOUNDED NO MORE

Two-Minute Takeaway (completed during session): _____
_____
_____

Observation from discussion with spouse (homework): _____
_____
_____

Action step—what God revealed that you need to contemplate or do (homework): _____
_____
_____

SESSION 3: OVERCOMING THE LIES OF THE ENEMY

Two-Minute Takeaway (completed during session): _____
_____
_____

Observation from discussion with spouse (homework): _____
_____
_____

Action step—what God revealed that you need to contemplate or do (homework): _____
_____
_____

SESSION 4: THE SAVAGE HELPER

Two-Minute Takeaway (completed during session): _____
_____
_____

Observation from discussion with spouse (homework): _____
_____
_____

Action step—what God revealed that you need to contemplate or do (homework): _____
_____
_____

SESSION 5: EXPERIENCING SPIRITUAL INTIMACY

Two-Minute Takeaway (completed during session): _____
_____
_____

Observation from discussion with spouse (homework): _____
_____
_____

Action step—what God revealed that you need to contemplate or do (homework): _____
_____
_____

SESSION 6: CREATING EMOTIONAL INTIMACY

Two-Minute Takeaway (completed during session): _____
_____
_____

Observation from discussion with spouse (homework): _____

_____

Action step—what God revealed that you need to contemplate or do (homework): _____

_____

SESSION 7: CHERISHING YOUR SPOUSE

Two-Minute Takeaway (completed during session): _____

_____

Observation from discussion with spouse (homework): _____

_____

Action step—what God revealed that you need to contemplate or do (homework): _____

_____

SESSION 8: BECOMING A GIVER, NOT A TAKER

Two-Minute Takeaway (completed during session): _____

_____

Observation from discussion with spouse (homework): _____

_____

Action step—what God revealed that you need to contemplate or do (homework): _____

_____

SESSION 9: BECOMING BATTLE PARTNERS

Two-Minute Takeaway (completed during session): _____

_____

Observation from discussion with spouse (homework): _____

_____

Action step—what God revealed that you need to contemplate or do (homework): _____

_____

NEXT SAVAGE STEPS!

Although this *Savage Marriage Study Guide* is concluded, your savage marriage journey with God continues!

Over years of watching people move on from Savage Marriage small groups, we've noticed one key difference between couples who experience success and those who don't.

> *Couples who diligently complete their action steps are most likely to experience a radically new, savage marriage.*

We encourage you to periodically revisit your action steps, reread some of the course materials, and ask God and your spouse to reveal how you're doing.

Also, join the Savage Community at savagemarriageministries.com to be notified of new Savage Marriage resources as they become available. Follow us on Instagram and Facebook @savagemarriageministries, and listen to the Savage Marriage podcasts on Spotify and iTunes. These resources will prompt interesting questions for you and your spouse to discuss and encourage you to continue developing your spiritual, emotional, and sexual intimacy.

Consider attending the weekend intensives offered by Whatever It Takes Ministries (witministries.com). They offer amazing weekend intensives designed for couples, women, and men. These life-changing weekends reinforce the concepts learned in this *Savage Marriage Study Guide* and provide opportunities for you to connect with like-minded couples. We frequently serve as coaches with Whatever It Takes Ministries and would love to see you there!

Finally, use your story of savage freedom to encourage and comfort others who may be going through storms in their marriages. When you do this, you will experience what the apostle Paul described when he said he would gladly boast about his weaknesses so the power of Christ may dwell in him (2 Cor. 12:9).

Our richest blessings to you and your generations that follow.

Phil and Priscilla Fretwell
407-342-4857 (Phil), 407-353-2920 (Priscilla)
phil.fretwell@savagemarriageministries.com
priscilla.fretwell@savagemarriageministries.com

Made in the USA
Las Vegas, NV
02 March 2025